A

The New York Times

NATION
CHALLENGED

Ground zero on September 11, 2001, at 10:14 a.m.

The New York Times
A NATION CHALLENGED
A VISUAL HISTORY OF 9/11 AND ITS AFTERMATH

INTRODUCTION BY HOWELL RAINES

PHOTOGRAPHS EDITED BY NANCY LEE AND LONNIE SCHLEIN

TEXT EDITED BY MITCHEL LEVITAS

ADDITIONAL TEXTS BY DAN BARRY, CELESTINE BOHLEN, JOHN F. BURNS AND N.R. KLEINFIELD

DESIGNED BY TOSHIYA MASUDA

JONATHAN CAPE

LONDON

September 10, 2001.

September 11, 2001.

March 11, 2002.   PHOTOGRAPHS BY DENTON TILLMAN

Contents

Moments before United Airlines Flight 175 strikes the south tower of the World Trade Center.

INTRODUCTION

HOWELL RAINES

That bright, blue Tuesday, September 11, was to be a busy day at The New York Times. There was a mayoral primary election to cover, and on Metro, assignment editors were at their desks early. When word came of the first plane hitting the first tower, photographers and reporters raced downtown.

Journalistic instinct and training dictated the initial response, but that day's story was a challenge no one could have predicted in those first minutes. As the hours ticked by, it turned into the tragedy of the World Trade Center, a story of death and destruction by terrorism that forever marked the lives of those who lived through it, covered it, read about it.

Americans watched the tragic day unfold in disbelief. At The Times, we drew on generations of tradition to move, to run, to cover the story that had exploded in our front yard and had immediately encompassed the world.

That morning began one of the largest mobilizations by The Times since World War II. Dozens of reporters and photographers converged on ground zero and the Pentagon as others moved out across America, Afghanistan, Pakistan and other crucial locations in Europe, the Middle East and Asia. What made this global crisis different for us at The Times is that it happened in our city. It

September 12, 8 p.m.

TYLER HICKS FOR NYT

was our story. We lived in the middle of it. The Times family lost loved ones. There were reporters here that first day who wrote while worrying about where their children or spouses were — or where their families would sleep that night. We pulled debris out of the hair of colleagues who had narrowly escaped the collapse.

But we knew the story was not about us. Our role was to be witnesses and reporters, detached professionals, yet understanding of the emotional pain of our fellow citizens and the public servants and their survivors and the families who suffered so grievously. Our task was to make sure that memories of these days would never fade. To a large degree, this book is a homage to those victims.

In devoting every resource we had to this story, which crossed all boundaries of politics and geography, we knocked down our own internal barriers. Science writers and editors worked with terrorism experts to write about anthrax. The Foreign Desk sent Metro and Washington reporters halfway around the world, to assignments they had never dreamed of.

It quickly became clear that a story this immense and far-reaching demanded a new approach in the telling, some creative way to be both comprehensive and coherent, to capture all the ripples and echoes from that one disastrous day. The solution, which grew organically out of the journalistic challenge before us, was a new free-standing section of the paper, A Nation Challenged. Introduced one week after the attacks, the section gave editors the freedom to show readers the breadth and depth of the unfolding story, and it gave us space for photographs and graphics unlike any ever before published in The Times. Many of the photographs and graphics in this book were displayed first on the full pages of the section, where accounts of the American war on terrorism in Afghanistan were juxtaposed against reports of the fighting in Afghanistan. The digging at ground zero, the anthrax scare, the Qaeda network, Washington's effort to enhance domestic security, the challenge to civil liberties: all were chronicled in great detail — and with unsparing intellectual balance — on those pages. At the end of the section, day after day, ran the Portraits of Grief, close to 2,000 brief stories of the lives of the missing at ground zero. These portraits, independently conceived and executed by our Metro Desk, became a national shrine.

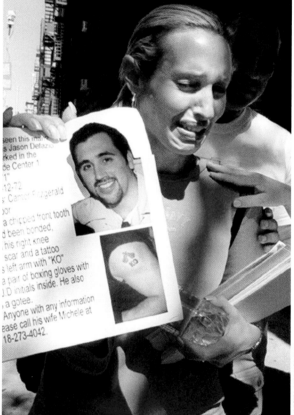

Michele Defazio holds a poster of her missing husband, Jason Defazio, who worked for Cantor Fitzgerald on the 104th floor of the north tower. September 13, 2001.

KRISTA NILES/NYT

Looking back, it is easy to impose some order on the pell-mell rush of events of the last months of 2001. On 9/11, the towers came down. Then the Pentagon was attacked and a fourth plane crashed in the fields of Pennsylvania. Suddenly the United States, so recently bounteous and self-involved, was besieged and worried. America confronted the general threat of terrorist attacks and a specific enemy that most citizens had never heard of until that day. Mayor Rudolph W. Giuliani of New York became a national symbol of resilience as he helped New Yorkers move on with their new lives. Soldiers prepared to fight the new enemy. Suddenly anthrax seemed to be loose in the mail, killing with a frightening lack of discrimination. And then there really was war.

None of this sequence of events was clear in the early days and weeks, and the ending, of course, remains hidden. As history keeps careering forward, we will record it. New stories will emerge to capture the nation's attention. Memories of these months will fade. Tales will be distorted in the retelling, and history altered with a shifting of priorities and the reordering of facts.

The pictures and text in this book, however, will remain for new generations, an unalterable record of our altered world. Not the vanished world of September 10. Not the world as the mullahs or the pundits or the Pentagon paint it or obscure it, or the world as we wish it could be, but the world in which this newspaper and its readers lived.

These photographs show, in James Agee's words, "the cruel radiance of what is." Let it be our tribute to those who did not live through these last turbulent months: a faithful record of the world they did not live to see.

United Airlines Flight 175 crashes into the south tower at 9:03 a.m.

I
SEPTEMBER 11, 2001

"All the News That's Fit to Print"

The New York Times

Late Edition

New York: Today, sunny, a few afternoon clouds. High 77. Tonight, slightly more humid. Low 65. Tomorrow, sun then clouds. High 81. Yesterday, high 81, low 63. Weather map, Page C19.

VOL. CL .. No. 51,874   Copyright © 2001 The New York Times   NEW YORK, WEDNESDAY, SEPTEMBER 12, 2001 $1 beyond the greater New York metropolitan area.   75 CENTS

U.S. ATTACKED

HIJACKED JETS DESTROY TWIN TOWERS AND HIT PENTAGON IN DAY OF TERROR

A CREEPING HORROR

Buildings Burn and Fall as Onlookers Search for Elusive Safety

By N. R. KLEINFIELD

It kept getting worse.

The horror arrived in episodic bursts of chilling disbelief, signified first by trembling floors, sharp eruptions, cracked windows. There was the actual unfathomable realization of a gaping, flaming hole in first one of the tall towers, and then the same thing all over again in its twin. There was the merciless sight of bodies helplessly tumbling out, some of them in flames.

Finally, the mighty towers themselves were reduced to nothing. Dense plumes of smoke raced through the downtown avenues, coursing between the buildings, shaped like tornadoes on their sides.

Every sound was cause for alarm. A plane appeared overhead. Was another one coming? No, it was a fighter jet. But was it friend or enemy? People scrambled for their lives, but they didn't know where to go. Should they go north, south, east, west? Stay outside, go indoors? People hid beneath cars and each other. Some contemplated jumping into the river.

For those trying to flee the very epicenter of the collapsing World Trade Center towers, the most horrid thought of all finally dawned on them: nowhere was safe.

For several panic-stricken hours yesterday morning, people in Lower Manhattan witnessed the inexpressible, the incomprehensible, the unthinkable. "I don't know what the gates of hell look like, but it's got to be like this," said John Maloney, a security director for an Internet firm in the trade center. "I'm a combat veteran, Vietnam, and I never saw anything like this."

The first warnings were small ones. Blocks away, Jim Farmer, a film composer, was having breakfast at a small restaurant on West Broadway. He heard the sound of a jet. An odd sound — too loud, it seemed, to be

Continued on Page A7

A Somber Bush Says Terrorism Cannot Prevail

By ELISABETH BUMILLER with DAVID E. SANGER

WASHINGTON, Sept. 11 — President Bush vowed tonight to retaliate against those responsible for today's attacks on New York and Washington, declaring that he would "make no distinction between the terrorists who committed these acts and those who harbor them."

"These acts of mass murder were intended to frighten our nation into chaos and retreat, but they have failed," the president said in his first speech to the nation from the Oval Office. "Our country is strong. Terrorist acts can shake the foundation of our biggest buildings, but they cannot touch the foundation of America."

His speech came after a day of trauma that seems destined to define his presidency. Seeking to at once calm the nation and declare his determination to exact retribution, he told a country numbed by repeated scenes of carnage that "these acts shattered steel, but they cannot dent the steel of American resolve."

Mr. Bush spoke only hours after returning from a zigzag course across the country, as his Secret Service and military security teams moved him from Florida, where he woke up this morning expecting to press for his education bill, to command posts in Louisiana and Nebraska before it was determined that the attacks had probably ended and he could safely return to the capital.

It was a sign of the catastrophic

Continued on Page A4

AMERICAN TARGETS A ball of fire exploded outward after the second of two jetliners slammed into the World Trade Center; less than two hours later, both of the 110-story towers were gone. Hijackers crashed a third airliner into the Pentagon, setting off a huge explosion and fire.

President Vows to Exact Punishment for 'Evil'

By SERGE SCHMEMANN

Hijackers rammed jetliners into each of New York's World Trade Center towers yesterday, toppling both in a hellish storm of ash, glass, smoke and leaping victims, while a third jetliner crashed into the Pentagon in Virginia. There was no official count, but President Bush said thousands had perished, and in the immediate aftermath the calamity was already being ranked the worst and most audacious terror attack in American history.

The attacks seemed carefully coordinated. The hijacked planes were all en route to California, and therefore gorged with fuel, and their departures were spaced within an hour and 40 minutes. The first, American Airlines Flight 11, a Boeing 767 out of Boston for Los Angeles, crashed into the north tower at 8:48 a.m. Eighteen minutes later, United Airlines Flight 175, also headed from Boston to Los Angeles, plowed into the south tower.

Then an American Airlines Boeing 757, Flight 77, left Washington's Dulles International Airport bound for Los Angeles, but instead hit the western part of the Pentagon, the military headquarters where 24,000 people work, at 9:40 a.m. Finally, United Airlines Flight 93, a Boeing 757 flying from Newark to San Francisco, crashed near Pittsburgh, raising the possibility that its hijackers had failed in whatever their mission was.

SECOND PLANE United Airlines Flight 175 nearing the trade center's south tower.   Kelly Guenther for The New York Times

There were indications that the hijackers on at least two of the planes were armed with knives. Attorney General John Ashcroft told reporters in the evening that the suspects on Flight 11 were armed that way. And Barbara Olson, a television commentator who was traveling on American Flight 77, managed to reach her husband, Solicitor General Theodore Olson, by cell phone and to tell him that the hijackers were armed with knives and a box cutter.

In all, 266 people perished in the four planes and several score more were known dead elsewhere. Numerous firefighters, police officers and other rescue workers who responded to the initial disaster in Lower Manhattan were killed or injured when the buildings collapsed. Hundreds were treated for cuts, broken bones, burns and smoke inhalation.

But the real carnage was concealed for now by the twisted, smoking, ash-choked carcasses of the twin towers, in which thousands of people used to work on a weekday. The collapse of the towers caused another World Trade Center building to fall 7 hours later, and several

Continued on Page A14

Awaiting the Aftershocks

Washington and Nation Plunge Into Fight With Enemy Hard to Identify and Punish

By R. W. APPLE Jr.

WASHINGTON, Sept. 11 — Today's devastating and astonishingly well-coordinated attacks on the World Trade Center towers in New York and on the Pentagon outside of Washington plunged the nation into a warlike struggle against an enemy that will be hard to identify with certainty and hard to punish with precision.

News Analysis

The whole nation — to a degree the whole world — shook as hijacked airliners plunged into buildings that symbolize the financial and military might of the United States. The sense of security and self-confidence that Americans take as their birthright suffered a grievous blow, from which recovery will be slow. The aftershocks will be nearly as bad, as hundreds and possibly thousands of people discover that friends or relatives died awful, fiery deaths.

Scenes of chaos and destruction evocative of the nightmare world of Hieronymus Bosch, with smoke and debris blotting out the sun, were carried by television into homes and workplaces across the nation. Echoing Franklin D. Roosevelt's description of the attack on Pearl Harbor as an event "which will live in infamy," Gov. George E. Pataki of New York, a Republican, and Senator Charles E. Schumer of New York, a Democrat, spoke of "a dastardly attack."

But mere words were inadequate vessels to contain the sense of shock and horror that people felt.

As Washington struggled to regain a sense of equilibrium, with warplanes and heavily armed helicopters crossing overhead, past and present national security officials earnestly debated the possibility of a Congressional declaration of war — but against precisely whom, and in what exact circumstances? Warships were maneuvering to protect New York and Washington. The North American Air Defense Command, which had seemed to many a relic of the cold war, adopted a pos-

Continued on Page A24

MORE ON THE ATTACKS

RESCUERS BECOME VICTIMS Firefighters who rushed to the trade center were killed. **PAGE A2**

SEARCH FOR SURVIVORS Some people trapped in the rubble for hours were rescued. **PAGE A2**

OFFICIALS SUSPECT BIN LADEN Eavesdropping intercepts after the attacks were cited. **PAGE A21**

TERRORISTS EXPLOIT WEAKNESS Investigators had criticized precautions against hijacking. **PAGE A17**

CASUALTIES IN WASHINGTON An unknown number of people were killed at the Pentagon. **PAGE A5**

Front page of the September 12, 2001, New York Times.

THE UNIMAGINABLE

N.R. KLEINFIELD

It was a late-summer day that at first seemed too beautiful and that almost at once became too awful. People were out in shirt sleeves and thin fabrics, enjoying the balmy air and the crystalline sky, some of them lazily on their way to polling places. It was Primary Day in the New York City mayoral election, but why hurry in this weather? Within the space of two hours, everything became almost too horrible to believe and impossible to forget. First there was the sound, the all-too-familiar everyday sound: a plane overhead. But even in this noisiest of cities, the sound was too loud, the plane much too low. And then the reason. The jetliner slammed high into the north tower of the World Trade Center, sounding to those nearby like a nasty auto accident, although the earth shook. It was 8:46 a.m., and some people had not even woken up.

People on the sidewalks gazed and gaped at the flames and smoke pouring out of the

View from East 25th Street.

jagged hole in the building's skin, their seesawing emotions challenging their capacity to absorb what was happening. It was stupefying, too much like a scene excerpted from the action movie of the week, as witnesses would later remark. Before sight and sound could entirely register, just 16 minutes later, the second plane rammed into the tower's twin and blew up in another hellacious ball of fire and smoke, and everyone knew the awful truth. This was no accident, but an audacious, carefully scripted terrorist attack.

The unreal yielded to the unimaginable. Specks appeared fluttering from the highest floors of the building; they had to be birds but astonishingly they were people leaping to their deaths, dresses and pants fluttering in the air currents, some of the jumpers with clasped hands in the swift descent. A firefighter died when a falling man landed on him. Bystanders gasped. Some retched.

Not much time would pass, not quite an hour. Then came the low rumble, and the brilliant sky quickly darkened, as if someone had shut off the sun. There was no light anywhere. It was morning but the sky was night. The once-mighty south tower began to come down upon itself. There was a loud whooshing sound as billowing black smoke roared down the surrounding streets, and no one could tell if the building itself was in the smoke, or just its ashes. The streets vibrated. Concrete, glass, steel, the entirety of a skyscraper, rained downward. Thousands panicked; blinded and gasping for breath, they ran for their lives. Women ran out of their shoes. People dropped briefcases, purses, cellphones. Ash coated their clothing and their skin, giving them the costumed look of apparitions. As they fled, people scooped up water bottles from abandoned vendor carts and poured it on themselves. Business paper was everywhere, curling into the bordering boroughs of Brooklyn, Queens and Staten Island. Chunks of the tower cascaded through the windows of offices and apartment buildings, left open to collect the morning's warmth. A computer flew out of the sky and plopped on a bed in a nearby apartment.

Once the smoke had lifted, as people brushed the dust off their clothes and out of their hair, there was this void. It was a stunning sight for it was the sight of nothing — emptiness where the tower had stood. People kept thinking, it was there, they just couldn't see it. How could it not be there? By then an eerie stillness hung over the unthinkable. A hundred and ten floors condensed to rubble. Poof, gone in seconds. People were too numb to speak or understand. Twenty-nine minutes later, the same thing happened all over again, as the companion north tower buckled and imploded. The same smoke and downpour of debris, the same disbelief, the same emptiness. And the quiet. Everything was entirely too quiet. A jet engine lay on Church Street, several blocks north of the fallen towers.

The attack was too great to grasp. Nearly 3,000 people had been crushed, including hundreds of firefighters and police officers who had rushed up the stairwells in the selfless hope of getting others out. Yet now word spread that another plane had wounded the Pentagon. A fourth had crashed in Pennsylvania. Others were somewhere in the air and unaccounted for. Were they headed this way? Was anywhere safe? Not knowing the answers to the tragedy intensified the terror. Fighter jets protectively flew overhead but some onlookers feared they were killers, too. Spooked people, sick with worry, streamed over the Brooklyn Bridge in a frantic getaway. Nobody would attack Brooklyn, would they? But no one yet knew the enemy or the method in its madness.

In the communications capital of the world, people desperately tried to communicate, but the phone lines were overwhelmed and communication became impossible. Dazed survivors from the towers staggered along the streets, groggy with the disbelief of their own experience. People sat in parked cars, windows and doors flung open, the radio tuned to the news; dozens gathered around to hear word of what was happening, but everything was unclear and tentative. High anxiety surged everywhere and no one felt secure. Medical personnel roamed the streets in an impromptu blood drive, asking volunteers to come to the hospitals and give blood. Many did, and in the end there was too much blood for too few wounded.

On John Street, after the collapse of both towers.

JUSTIN LANE FOR NYT

And it was still morning, with a whole day left. During the disconnected, endless hours after the twin towers no longer existed, many people simply did not know what to do. They did not know where to go or what to say, how to be themselves. Their frame of reality had cracked. As they relived the unspeakable reaches of the event, they dared not dwell on the potential death toll. But people knew to hug their loved ones tighter and to look out for each other. Individual energies were channeled into a common good.

On the darkest day in the city's history, night fell on what was also a different city. It was weakened and numbed, yanked from its moorings, a frightened city of less. Its entrances were sealed and its planes grounded. People locked their doors and tried to keep calm when they heard the shriek of sirens. Lower Manhattan stood lower with its matching towers gone. The fires burned. In thousands and thousands of grieving homes, fathers and mothers and sons and daughters did not return. Now they knew death and had seen the face of evil.

United Airlines Flight 175 hits the south tower.

SEPTEMBER 11, 2001

The south tower explodes. In the foreground is the Brooklyn Bridge.

It was one of those moments in which history splits, and we define the world as "before" and "after."

— **EDITORIAL**
SEPTEMBER 12, 2001

For those trying to flee the very epicenter of the collapsing World Trade Center towers, the most horrid thought of all finally dawned on them: nowhere was safe.

—N.R. Kleinfield
September 12, 2001

A woman (near bottom, left of center) looks out from the north tower after it was hit.

The
Desperate Flight

When the first jet struck 1 World Trade Center at 8:46 a.m. on Tuesday, the people in 2 World Trade Center with a view of the instant inferno across the divide had the clearest sense of what they, too, must do: get out fast.

Katherine Ilachinski, who had been knocked off her chair by the blast of heat exploding from the neighboring tower, was one of those. Despite her 70 years, Ms. Ilachinski, an architect working on the 91st floor of 2 World Trade Center, the south tower, went for the stairs. Twelve floors above her, Judy Wein, an executive, screamed and set off too.

But others up and down the 110 floors, many without clear views of the damage across the way and thus unclear about what was happening, were not so sure. And the 16 minutes before the next plane would hit were ticking off.

Friends and colleagues, each offering a version of expertise or calm, debated the wisdom of leaving. Amid the uncertainty about what was the best thing to do, formal announcements inside the south tower instructed people to stay put, reassuring them that the building was sound and the threat was limited to the other tower.

Some left, others stayed. Some began the climb down and, when met with more announcements and other cautions to stop or return, went back up. The decisions made in those instants proved momentous, because many who opted to stay were doomed when the second jet crashed into the south tower, killing many and stranding many more in the floors above where the jet hit.

Without question, particularly at 1 World Trade Center, the north tower, the evacuation of thousands of people went well, with people helping each other with acts of courage great and modest.

People on floors as high as the 88th at the north tower, stepping over rubble, made the full trip to safety. In the packed stairwells, people stepped aside to let burn victims speed past. Firefighters rushed upward, assisting as they climbed.

Port Authority officials say that considerable numbers of people were evacuated within an hour, 30 minutes less than even their drills.

—**Michael Moss and Charles V. Bagli**
SEPTEMBER 13, 2001

RUTH FREMSON/NYT

On Vesey Street: After escaping the towers, people were not sure which way to run.

Evacuation at the base of the north tower.

People trapped on the upper levels of the north tower hang out the windows, calling for help.

NO ESCAPE

It kept getting worse.

The horror arrived in episodic bursts of chilling disbelief, signified first by trembling floors, sharp eruptions, cracked windows. There was the actual unfathomable realization of a gaping, flaming hole in first one of the tall towers, and then the same thing all over again in its twin. There was the merciless sight of bodies helplessly tumbling out, some of them in flames.

—N.R. KLEINFIELD
SEPTEMBER 12, 2001

A man falls from the north tower.

FIRE AND ASHES

RICHARD DREW/ASSOCIATED PRESS

Above and right: The south tower, the first one to fall, collapses at 9:59 a.m.

First, a sharp crack and then what sounded, oddly, like a waterfall, thousands of panes of glass shattering as the north side of the tower buckled. Then a slow, building rumble like rolling thunder that will not stop as the tower cascades toward the ground.

— **David Rohde**
SEPTEMBER 16, 2001

No building this high has ever collapsed.

— **Eduardo Kausel**
Massachusetts Institute of Technology
SEPTEMBER 12, 2001

The high temperatures, of perhaps 1,000 to 2,000 degrees, probably weakened the steel supports, the experts said, causing the external walls to buckle and allowing the floors above to fall almost straight down. That led to catastrophic failures of the rest of the buildings. "No structure could have sustained this kind of assault," says one expert.

— **James Glanz**
SEPTEMBER 12, 2001

SHOCK WAVES

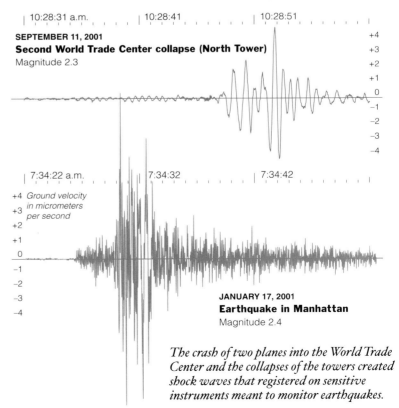

10:28:31 a.m. 10:28:41 10:28:51

SEPTEMBER 11, 2001
Second World Trade Center collapse (North Tower)
Magnitude 2.3

7:34:22 a.m. 7:34:32 7:34:42

Ground velocity in micrometers per second

JANUARY 17, 2001
Earthquake in Manhattan
Magnitude 2.4

The crash of two planes into the World Trade Center and the collapses of the towers created shock waves that registered on sensitive instruments meant to monitor earthquakes.

SOURCE: COLUMBIA UNIVERSITY'S LAMONT-DOHERTY EARTH OBSERVATORY   THE NEW YORK TIMES

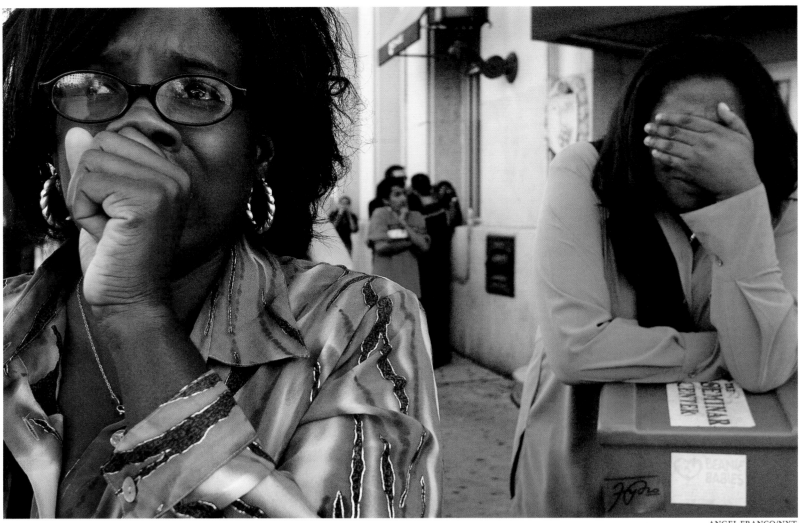

Watching the north tower collapse.

Witness to Horror

For several panic-stricken hours yesterday morning, people in Lower Manhattan witnessed the inexpressible, the incomprehensible, the unthinkable. "I don't know what the gates of hell look like, but it's got to be like this," said John Maloney, a security director for an Internet firm in the trade center. "I'm a combat veteran, Vietnam, and I never saw anything like this."

—**N.R. Kleinfield**
SEPTEMBER 12, 2001

People run from the collapse, down Fulton Street.

MARILYNN K. YEE/NYT

Barclay Street near West Broadway.

AMY SANCETTA/ASSOCIATED PRESS

Ann Street.

RUTH FREMSON/NYT

Church Street in front of Trinity Church.

The Brooklyn Bridge.

In front of Trinity Church.

Stage Door Deli on Vesey Street.

AFTERSHOCKS

New Yorkers were members of a tribe in shock, tied in knots and easily moved to sudden tears and swift kindnesses. People moved through Midtown without the ordinary get-out-of-my-way pace. They listened to radios. They grabbed one-minute updates from strangers. They spoke urgently into cellphones. They waited quietly in long lines — no shoving, no impatient words — at the pay phones on street corners. The hundreds who sat or stood under outdoor jumbo electronic television screens were virtually silent; it was no time for small talk.

—**JIM DWYER AND SUSAN SACHS**
SEPTEMBER 12, 2001

Volunteers helped themselves to Burger King hamburger buns, Starbucks biscotti, and any other food they could find in restaurants with shattered glass facades. Firefighters hosed down the elegant lobby of the American Express building on Vesey Street to wash away the dust permeating what had become an emergency trauma center.

—**DAN BARRY**
SEPTEMBER 13, 2001

S moke clears, and a wail: "Where did it go? Oh, Lord, where did it go?"

—N.R. KLEINFIELD
SEPTEMBER 12, 2001

The north tower falls at 10:28 a.m.

Anatomy of a Collapse

Following the attacks, engineers pieced together a likely sequence for the destruction at the World Trade Center. Published November 11, 2001.

The Critical Components

EXTERIOR COLUMNS

They provided about 40 percent of the support for the weight of the building, but their primary purpose was to stiffen the building against the wind.

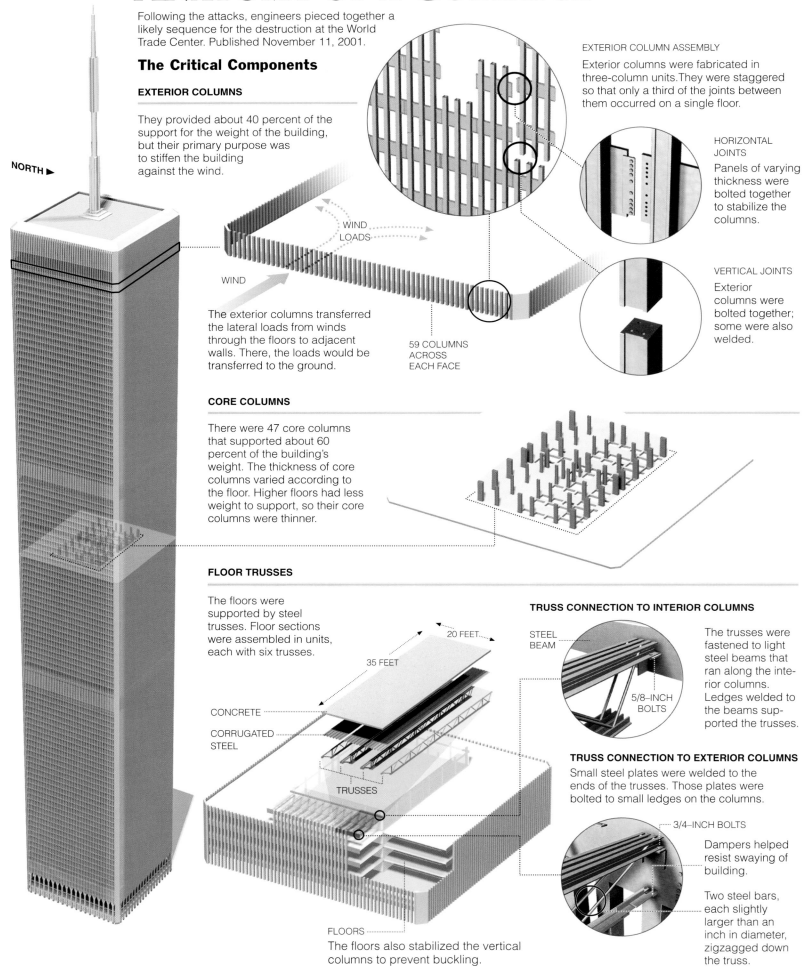

NORTH ►

WIND LOADS

WIND

The exterior columns transferred the lateral loads from winds through the floors to adjacent walls. There, the loads would be transferred to the ground.

59 COLUMNS ACROSS EACH FACE

EXTERIOR COLUMN ASSEMBLY

Exterior columns were fabricated in three-column units. They were staggered so that only a third of the joints between them occurred on a single floor.

HORIZONTAL JOINTS

Panels of varying thickness were bolted together to stabilize the columns.

VERTICAL JOINTS

Exterior columns were bolted together; some were also welded.

CORE COLUMNS

There were 47 core columns that supported about 60 percent of the building's weight. The thickness of core columns varied according to the floor. Higher floors had less weight to support, so their core columns were thinner.

FLOOR TRUSSES

The floors were supported by steel trusses. Floor sections were assembled in units, each with six trusses.

20 FEET

35 FEET

CONCRETE

CORRUGATED STEEL

TRUSSES

FLOORS
The floors also stabilized the vertical columns to prevent buckling.

TRUSS CONNECTION TO INTERIOR COLUMNS

STEEL BEAM

5/8–INCH BOLTS

The trusses were fastened to light steel beams that ran along the interior columns. Ledges welded to the beams supported the trusses.

TRUSS CONNECTION TO EXTERIOR COLUMNS

Small steel plates were welded to the ends of the trusses. Those plates were bolted to small ledges on the columns.

3/4–INCH BOLTS

Dampers helped resist swaying of building.

Two steel bars, each slightly larger than an inch in diameter, zigzagged down the truss.

Why the North Tower Fell

Though the two towers did not collapse in exactly the same way, a detailed look at the collapse of the north tower sheds light on the crucial elements of both collapses.

NORTH ▶

THE COLLISION WITH THE TOWER

At 8:46 a.m. a Boeing 767 with nearly 10,000 gallons of fuel onboard hits the north face, exerting a force equivalent to about 25 million pounds. A huge explosion and fire ensue.

AMERICAN
AIRLINES
FLIGHT 11

THE COLUMNS

The impact causes severe structural damage, blowing out some 35 exterior columns between floors 94 and 98 and obliterating portions of those floors. The impact also knocks loose some fireproofing on the columns and trusses.

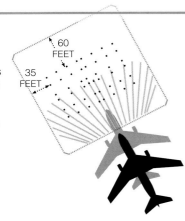

60 FEET

35 FEET

About a third of the impact's energy dissipates before pieces of the plane strike the core columns. Calculations suggest that no more than half of the core columns are seriously damaged.

98

IMPACT AREA **94**

VIERENDEEL TRUSS

Structural components above and adjacent to the damaged area begin to function like an arch — what engineers call a Vierendeel truss, transferring loads around the hole and downward through remaining columns at the sides. The building stands for 102 minutes, giving many people a chance to escape.

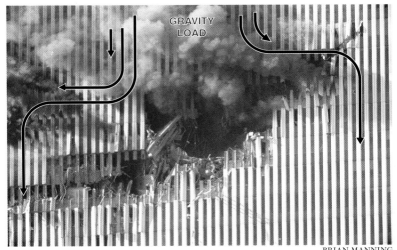

GRAVITY LOAD

BRIAN MANNING

Meanwhile, though, heat from the burning fuel and other materials raises temperatures to more than 1,100 degrees, the point at which steel begins losing its strength. Nearly 40,000 tons of building weight sit within and above the impact area.

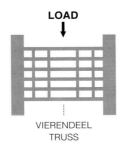

LOAD

VIERENDEEL TRUSS

THE FALL

❶ The steel trusses are particularly vulnerable to the fire, because their ratio of surface area to volume is large, causing them to heat up quickly. Extreme heat softens the steel and reduces its ability to support the floors.

❷ Having lost their lateral support, the exterior columns, already softened by the fire, buckle catastrophically.

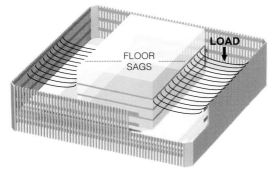

FLOOR SAGS

LOAD

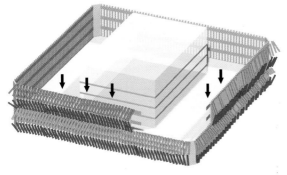

As the floors weaken, they tug at their connections, which tear away from the core and exterior columns.

The top portion of the building plummets, and the building collapses in roughly 12 seconds. A stone dropped from the top of the tower would have taken 9.2 seconds to fall to the ground.

Sources: Leslie E. Robertson Associates; Port Authority; Skilling Ward Magnusson Barkshire; Dr. Yogesh Jaluria, Rutgers University; Dr. Eduardo Kausel, M.I.T.; Dr. Tomasz Wierzbicki, M.I.T.; International Federation of Air Line Dispatchers' Associations

STEVE DUENES AND MIKA GRÖNDAHL/NYT

The Woolworth Building stands tall after the collapse of ~ World Trade Center at 5:28 p.m.

TING-LI WANG/NYT

Firefighters work amid the debris from 7 World Trade Center.

View from the Cortlandt Street subway station.

AMONG THE RUINS

These acts shattered steel, but they cannot dent the steel of American resolve.

— **PRESIDENT GEORGE W. BUSH**
SEPTEMBER 12, 2001

"The entire block is incinerated. It doesn't look like anything you would be able to pull anybody out of."

—**Dr. David Nagel**
New York University Downtown Hospital
SEPTEMBER 16, 2001

Firefighters from Ladder 21 embrace a colleague who cannot find a family member and fellow firefighter.

Rescue workers carry the body of Mychal F. Judge, the Franciscan Friar who was Chaplain of the Fire Department of New York City.

Unspeakable Loss

Shaken firefighters and officers spent much of the day searching through the rubble for lost colleagues, mourning and rearranging responsibilities as they attempted to deal with the loss of so many senior people.

— **Kevin Flynn**
SEPTEMBER 13, 2001

Sep. 12, 2001, 17:37:19   impact

Sep. 12, 2001, 17:37:21   #2 impact

Sep. 12, 2001, 17:37:22   #3 impact

Sep. 12, 2001, 17:37:23   #4 impact

Footage from a Pentagon surveillance camera. Because of a system malfunction, the incorrect date and time appear on the image.

ATTACK ON THE PENTAGON

Many of the Pentagon's more than 20,000 civilians and military personnel were already on edge when the attack came. News of the crashes at the trade center had shot through the corridors and it seemed as if every office television was turned on. Military and civilian employees watched in disbelief as smoke engulfed the two towers.

In a macabre foreshadowing of what then happened, Mike Slater, a former Marine, told his coworkers, "We're next."

Then the Pentagon, built to withstand terrorist attacks, shook like a rickety roller coaster. A section of it collapsed and burned. "It sounded like a roar," said Mr. Slater, who was 500 yards away from where the jet slammed into the Pentagon's west side. "I knew it was a bomb or something."

— **DON van NATTA AND LIZETTE ALVAREZ**
SEPTEMBER 12, 2001

Today's devastating and astonishingly well-coordinated attacks on the World Trade Center towers in New York and on the Pentagon outside of Washington plunged the nation into a warlike struggle against an enemy that will be hard to identify with certainty and hard to punish with precision.

— **R.W. APPLE JR.**
SEPTEMBER 12, 2001

On September 11, American Airlines Flight 77 crashed into the Pentagon, one of the world's most secure military installations. Fires continued to burn in the western side of the Pentagon on September 12, but more than half of the offices were open.

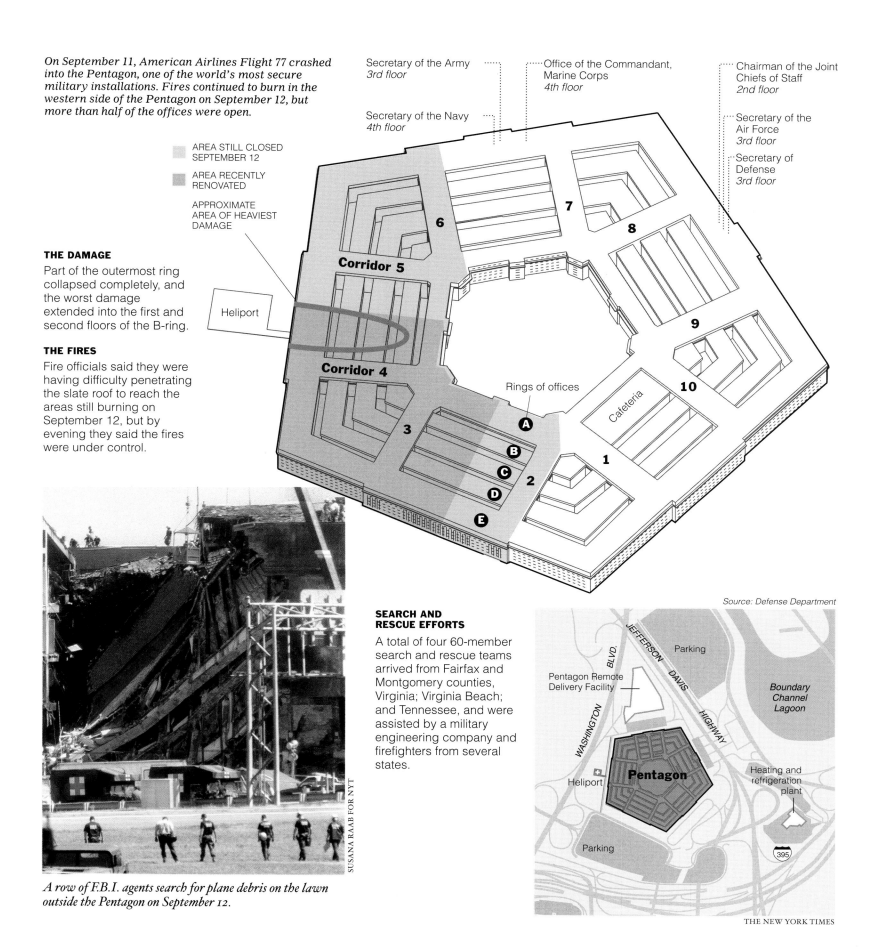

Secretary of the Army
3rd floor

Office of the Commandant, Marine Corps
4th floor

Chairman of the Joint Chiefs of Staff
2nd floor

Secretary of the Navy
4th floor

Secretary of the Air Force
3rd floor

Secretary of Defense
3rd floor

AREA STILL CLOSED SEPTEMBER 12

AREA RECENTLY RENOVATED

APPROXIMATE AREA OF HEAVIEST DAMAGE

THE DAMAGE

Part of the outermost ring collapsed completely, and the worst damage extended into the first and second floors of the B-ring.

THE FIRES

Fire officials said they were having difficulty penetrating the slate roof to reach the areas still burning on September 12, but by evening they said the fires were under control.

Heliport

Corridor 5

Corridor 4

Rings of offices

Cafeteria

6   7   8   9   10

A   B   C   D   E

3   2   1

Source: Defense Department

SEARCH AND RESCUE EFFORTS

A total of four 60-member search and rescue teams arrived from Fairfax and Montgomery counties, Virginia; Virginia Beach; and Tennessee, and were assisted by a military engineering company and firefighters from several states.

JEFFERSON DAVIS HIGHWAY

WASHINGTON BLVD.

Parking

Pentagon Remote Delivery Facility

Boundary Channel Lagoon

Heliport

Pentagon

Heating and refrigeration plant

Parking

395

A row of F.B.I. agents search for plane debris on the lawn outside the Pentagon on September 12.

THE NEW YORK TIMES

VICTIMS FIGHT BACK

They told the people they loved that they would die fighting.

In a series of cellular telephone calls to their wives, two passengers aboard the plane that crashed into a Pennsylvania field instead of possibly toppling a national landmark learned about the horror of the World Trade Center. From 35,000 feet, they relayed harrowing details about the hijacking in progress to the police. And they vowed to try to thwart the enemy, to prevent others from dying even if they could not save themselves.

The accounts revealed a spirit of defiance amid the desperation. Relatives and friends and a congressman who represents the area around the crash site in Pennsylvania hailed the fallen passengers as the patriots of America's darkest day.

"Apparently they made enough of a difference that the plane did not complete its mission," said Lyzbeth Glick's [passenger Jeremy Glick's widow] uncle, Tom Crowley, of Atlanta. In an e-mail message forwarded far and wide, Mr. Crowley urged: "May we remember Jeremy and the other brave souls as heroes, soldiers and Americans on United Flight 93 who so gallantly gave their lives to save many others."

—**JODI WILGOREN AND EDWARD WONG**
SEPTEMBER 13, 2001

*Firefighters and emergency personnel at the scene of the crash of
United Airlines Flight 93, about 80 miles southeast of Pittsburgh.*

American Flight 11

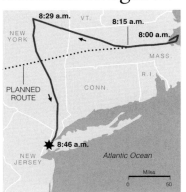

8:29 a.m.
8:15 a.m.
8:00 a.m.
NEW YORK
VT.
MASS.
CONN.
R.I.
PLANNED ROUTE
NEW JERSEY
Atlantic Ocean
8:46 a.m.
Miles 0 50

8:00:00 Plane takes off from Boston, headed for Los Angeles.

8:13 Boston Control Center: **"AAL11 turn 20 degrees right."**
AAL11: **"20 right AAL11."**
Controller: **"AAL11 now climb, maintain FL350 [35,000 feet]."**
Controller: **"AAL11 climb, maintain FL350."**
Controller: **"AAL11 Boston."**

8:14:33 Controller A: **"AAL11, ah, the American on the frequency, how do you hear me?"**
Controller B: **"This is, uh, Athens."**
A: **"This is Boston. I turned American 20 left and I was going to climb him. He will not respond to me now at all."**
B: **"Looks like he's turning right."**
A: **"Yea, I turned him right."**
B: **"Oh, O.K."**
A: **"And he's only going to, um, I think 29."**
B: **"Sure, that's fine."**
A: **"Eh, but I'm not talking to him."**
B: **"He won't answer you. He's nordo [no radio] roger. Thanks."**

8:24:38 Hijackers' voices heard: **"We have some planes. Just stay quiet and you will be O.K. We are returning to the airport. Nobody move, everything will be O.K. If you try to make any moves, you'll endanger yourself and the airplane. Just stay quiet."**

8:25:00 The control tower notifies several air traffic control centers that a hijacking is in progress.

8:33:59 Hijackers' voices heard: **"Nobody move please, we are going back to the airport. Don't try to make any stupid moves."**

United Flight 175

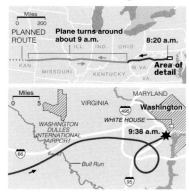

VERMONT
NEW HAMPSHIRE
8:14 a.m.
MASSACHUSETTS
NEW YORK
CONN.
R.I.
PLANNED ROUTE
8:47 a.m.
9:03 a.m.
PA.
NEW JERSEY
Atlantic Ocean
Miles 0 50

8:14:00 Plane takes off from Boston, headed for Los Angeles.

8:31:04 Flight makes contact with Boston control center.

8:37:08 Controller asks pilots to look for a lost American Airlines plane: **"Do you have traffic? Look at, uh, your 12 to 1 o'clock at about, uh, 10 miles southbound to see if you can see an American seventy sixty seven out there please."**
UAL175: **"Affirmative. We have him, uh, he looks, uh, about 20, yeah, about 29, 28,000."**
Controller: **"United 175, turn 5 turn 30 degrees to the right. I [want to] keep you away from this traffic."**

8:41:32 Cockpit: **"We figured we'd wait to go to your center. We heard a suspicious transmission on our departure out of Boston. Someone keyed the mike and said, 'Everyone stay in your seats.'"**
Cockpit: **"Did you copy that?"**
Flight turns toward the southwest, with clearance from air traffic control.

American Flight 77

Miles 0 200
PLANNED ROUTE
Plane turns around about 9 a.m.
ILL. IND. OHIO
8:20 a.m.
KAN.
MISSOURI
KENTUCKY
W.VA.
VA.
Area of detail

Miles 0 5
VIRGINIA
MARYLAND
Washington
495
WHITE HOUSE
9:38 a.m.
66
WASHINGTON DULLES INTERNATIONAL AIRPORT
Bull Run
95

8:20:00 Plane takes off from Dulles airport, headed for Los Angeles.

8:25:49 Plane is instructed to climb to 27,000 feet.

8:37:33 Plane is instructed to climb to 39,000 feet, but the pilot requests and is granted a cruising altitude of 35,000 feet.

8:50:51 Last radio communication with aircraft.

United Flight 93

CANADA
NEW YORK
9:36 a.m.
8:42 a.m.
PENNSYLVANIA
PLANNED ROUTE
10:06 a.m.
OHIO
N.J.
MD.
DEL.
W. VA.
VIRGINIA
Miles 0 100

8:42:00 Plane takes off from Newark, headed for San Francisco.

At some point after 8:53, a flight dispatcher at a United operations center in Chicago sends out a text message to 15 planes, including Flight 93, that there had been a cockpit intrusion on another United flight. Flight 93 responds that the message was received.

9:00 9:10 9:20 9:30 9:40 9:50 10:00

8:46:26 Plane crashes into the north tower of the World Trade Center.

VOICES FROM THE SKY

The drama and terror of September 11 unfolded over air traffic control frequencies from New Hampshire to Virginia, from Ohio to Long Island. Excerpts were prepared for investigators from transcripts of audiotapes at the control centers that communicated with the four planes. All times are Eastern Daylight.

Key

 Takeoff

 Last routine communication

 First deviation from flight plan

 Military air defense notified that plane is hijacked

 Crash

8:53:23 Controller: **"We may have a hijack. We have some problems over here right now."**

9:00:02 Last radar reading is observed at an altitude of 18,000 feet as the flight is descending at a ground speed of 550 miles per hour.

9:02:54 Plane crashes into the south tower of the World Trade Center.

9:02:17 On a second call to American Airlines, the controller says, **"We, uh, we lost track control of the guy. He's in coast track but we haven't — we don't know really where his target [radar location] is, and we can't get a hold of him. Um, you guys tried him and no response. ... Yeah, we have no radar contact and, uh, no communications with him, so if you guys can try again."**
Dispatcher: **"We're doing it."**
Controller: **"All right. Thanks a lot."**

9:06:31 Controller: **"You guys never been able to raise him at all."**
Another controller: **"No, we called company. They can't even get a hold of him. So there's no, no radar, uh, no radio communications and no radar."**

9:25 Controller observes the plane moving toward Washington.

9:33 Controller informs Operational Supervisor, who in turn informs the Secret Service. The aircraft is observed completing a right 360-degree turn, just south of the Pentagon.

9:36 National Airport instructs a military C-130 that had just departed Andrews Air Force Base to intercept and identify it. The C-130 reports it is a Boeing 767, moving low and very fast.

9:38 Plane crashes into the southwest side of the Pentagon.

9:28:19 First audible sign of problems in background cockpit noise.

9:35:09 Plane climbs without authorization.

Sometime after 9:30, two passengers make the first of several calls to their wives, saying that three or four passengers are discussing how they may stop the hijackers. One man on the plane also speaks directly to 911 dispatchers, relaying details of a hijacking in progress. Several other passengers on the flight place cellphone calls. Investigators who have heard the cockpit voice recorder have described the sounds of a struggle taking place.

10:00:00 Controller states: **"Think he is at 7,500 [feet]."**

10:06:00 Controller calls controller on land line to say Flight 93 is down.

GRAPHIC BY BADEN COPELAND, HANNAH FAIRFIELD, SARAH SLOBIN, HUGH TRUSLOW AND ARCHIE TSE

MORNING OF MAYHEM

By 8 a.m. on September 11, a chain of events had been set in motion that, two hours later, would erase the World Trade Center towers from the New York City skyline, rip open the west wall of the Pentagon, drop four planes from the sky and kill 3,049 people. Following is a look at how events unfolded. All times are Eastern Daylight.

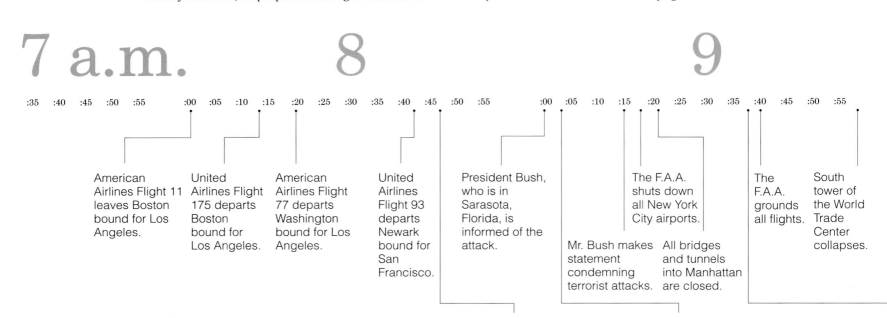

7 a.m. 8 9

:35 :40 :45 :50 :55 :00 :05 :10 :15 :20 :25 :30 :35 :40 :45 :50 :55 :00 :05 :10 :15 :20 :25 :30 :35 :40 :45 :50 :55

American Airlines Flight 11 leaves Boston bound for Los Angeles.

United Airlines Flight 175 departs Boston bound for Los Angeles.

American Airlines Flight 77 departs Washington bound for Los Angeles.

United Airlines Flight 93 departs Newark bound for San Francisco.

President Bush, who is in Sarasota, Florida, is informed of the attack.

The F.A.A. shuts down all New York City airports.

Mr. Bush makes statement condemning terrorist attacks.

All bridges and tunnels into Manhattan are closed.

The F.A.A. grounds all flights.

South tower of the World Trade Center collapses.

Flight 11 hits the north tower of the World Trade Center.

Flight 175 strikes the south tower of the World Trade Center.

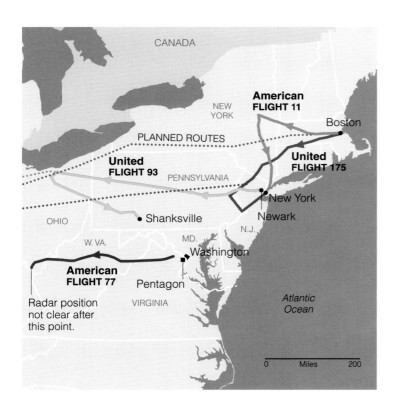

10   11   12 p.m.   1

:00 :05 :10 :15 :20 :25 :30 :35 :40 :45 :50 :55   :00 :05 :10 :15 :20 :25 :30 :35 :40 :45 :50 :55   :00 :05 :10 :15 :20 :25 :30 :35 :40 :45 :50 :55   :00 :05 :10 :15 :20 :25 :30 :35 :40 :45 :50 :55

White House is evacuated.

President Bush leaves Sarasota.

All incoming international flights are diverted to Canada.

New York City primary elections are canceled.

North tower of the World Trade Center collapses.

Mayor Rudolph W. Giuliani orders an evacuation of Manhattan south of Canal Street.

U.N. head-quarters in New York is fully evacuated.

Los Angeles International airport, the original destination of three of the flights, is evacuated and closed.

San Francisco International airport is evacuated and closed.

President Bush speaks from Barksdale Air Force Base in Louisiana.

Reuters

Pentagon announces that warships and aircraft carriers will take up positions in the New York and Washington areas.

10:10 — A portion of the Pentagon collapses.

10:06 — Flight 93 crashes in Shanksville, 80 miles southeast of Pittsburgh.

Flight 77 hits the Pentagon.

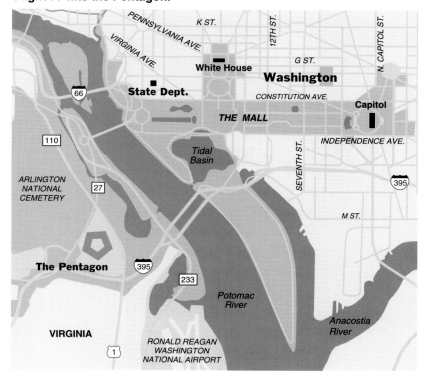

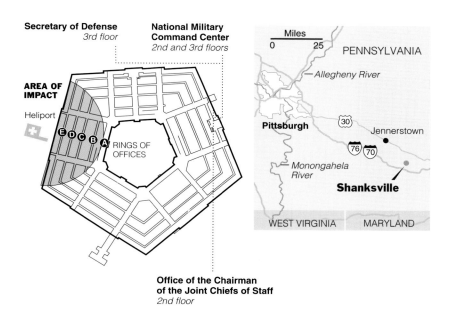

Secretary of Defense
3rd floor

National Military Command Center
2nd and 3rd floors

AREA OF IMPACT

Heliport

E D C B A   RINGS OF OFFICES

Office of the Chairman of the Joint Chiefs of Staff
2nd floor

Sources: Various wire reports; Defense Department; Flytecomm; Flight Explorer

Bearing Witness

'I Heard the Plane'

NATALIA LESZ, *a 21-year-old student staying in a hotel in Union Square while her apartment was being renovated, was on the phone with her mother in Warsaw:*
"I called my mom at 9 a.m. and was talking about a guy I met. I speak to my mother every morning. Then my dog, Izzy, a Maltese, raised his head. I heard the plane in the seventh floor of the W hotel. I told her 'I think a plane is next to my window.'"

First Plane Hits

GREGORY DOWNER *was walking his dog at Fifth Avenue and 11th Street:*
"There were 12 people. We all looked up. We all thought it would be unusual for a plane to be flying so low over the city.
"It scooped down even lower over the South Village — almost like a missile — and then toward the north tower of the World Trade Center. When it went into the building we all screamed — we couldn't believe what we saw."

LAKSHMAN ACHUTHAN, *managing director of the Economic Cycle Research Institute, was at a meeting at 1 World Trade Center:*
"The breakfast started at 8 and at about 8:50 Robert Scott, who is Morgan Stanley's president, was speaking. Then there is this thud and you could see everyone's face just widen up."

LYNN SIMPSON, *communications director of Strategic Communications Group, was on the 89th floor of 1 World Trade Center:*
"I heard an enormous crash. The ceiling fell in, the lights went out and the sprinklers went on. There was a fire in the stairwell. I told everyone to get out.
"We went into a side office and we were listening to the radio — some talk show — and the D.J.'s were joking, saying a kamikaze pilot has crashed into the World Trade Center and they were laughing. We thought we were going to die."

LEONORE MCKEAN, *a paralegal at Merrill Lynch, was working at 222 Broadway, near Barclay Street, when her building shook and she heard a terrible crash:*
"We saw people jumping from high windows at the World Trade Center. It was so crushing. I suppose if you had to choose between burning to death and falling unconscious, which would you choose?"

EDGARDO VILLAGAS *hurried down 32 flights of steps in 2 World Trade Center and arrived outside to the view of people in midair:*
"They looked like rag dolls being tossed. Their bodies were lifeless; just twirling in the air, dressed in suits."

Between Crashes

SHARNISE WINGATE, *25, a service technician for Verizon, was making a repair call in Brooklyn Heights when a friend called her to tell her that one of the towers had been hit:*
"I was watching the flames and saw a second aircraft come in low and make a sharp left into the second tower. I was confused. It didn't look like a rescue aircraft."

LISLE TAYLOR *was on her way to work at Goldman Sachs:*
"I got out of the subway and there were hundreds of pieces of paper in the air. I thought it was a marketing campaign. Then I heard a boom."

GEORGE C. SHEA, *37, was driving north, just out of the Brooklyn-Battery Tunnel, when a blue-gray sport utility vehicle in front of him was hit by an enormous wheel that he believes was from a plane:*
"I'm guessing 8 or 10 feet in diameter, in a rain of debris, with a strut, prop, metal attached to it."

Towers Collapse

JIM ZAMPARELLI, *54, was standing near Stuyvesant High School:*
"This is the most horrifying thing I've ever experienced. Look — Oh, my God, look — there's a person falling. I can't watch. Don't watch. Oh my God, as we're talking that whole tower is falling. Run!"

KEITH VANCE, *33, had been standing on Broadway in front of Trinity Church when he saw the tower collapse:*
"I was surprised how long it lasted. It was probably only 30 seconds, but it felt like five minutes."

Fleeing the Scene

MIKE DIAZ PIEDRA'S *leg was broken when he was trampled in the garage of 75 Park Place after the first plane hit:*
"All of a sudden, people went crazy. And then a man built like a refrigerator ran over me."

MARCI UIHLEIN, *from San Franciso, and her boyfriend, Joe Morris, had just entered the New York Stock Exchange when the first plane hit:*
"All of my life, I've wanted to come and see New York City. Now, I want desperately to figure how to get out."

Beyond the Blast

MALKIE YADAIE, *the owner of Ben-Ness Photos on University Place, said that people rushed in to buy disposable cameras:*
"Some didn't wait for their change, just ran out. Some were screaming."

ESTHER ALLEN *went to Public School 41 on West 11th Street to pick up her two sons and found that evacuees from Public School 234, three blocks north of the trade center, had been brought there. She volunteered to stay with a class of those children:*
"They were shellshocked. I tried to be lively and happy with them, but no, they had seen a lot."

Victims and Rescuers

RICHARD VITALE, *a firefighter with Ladder Company 24, took the Staten Island Ferry to the scene and ran toward where the World Trade Center used to be:*
"There were body parts everywhere. You couldn't tell the body parts from the metal."

JOE LENNON, *a four-year veteran of the Fire Department, had to fight back tears:*
"You lose one guy and that is major. To lose 200-plus brothers — it's not easy."

THE REV. LLOYD PRATOR *stood on the sidewalk to meet the ambulances to bless victims and give last rites:*
"It was a glimpse of hell. People were covered with debris and glass. Everyone was covered with ash."

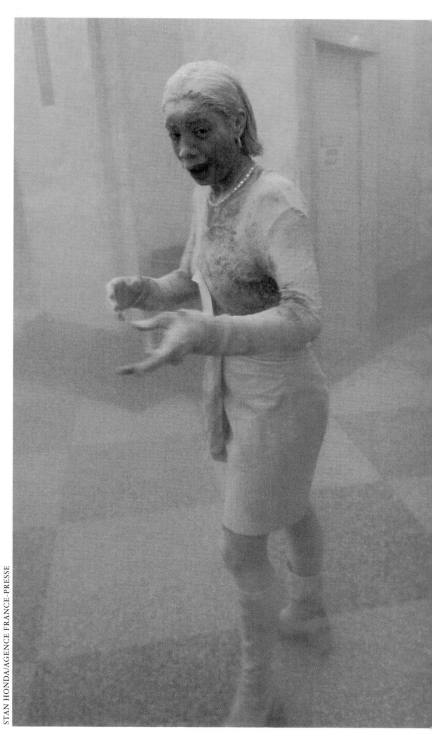

STAN HONDA/AGENCE FRANCE-PRESSE

Marcy Borders, who descended from the 81st floor of the north tower, takes refuge in an office building on lower Broadway after the collapse of the World Trade Center.

WORLD REACTION

EUROPE

EUROPEAN UNION — European foreign ministers scheduled a rare emergency meeting for today to discuss a joint response, as officials expressed solidarity with the United States. The external relations commissioner, Chris Patten, called the attacks "the work of a madman."

Prime Minister Tony Blair

BRITAIN — British security forces across the world were placed on maximum alert. Prime Minister Tony Blair pledged that Britain would stand "full square alongside the U.S." in the battle against terrorism. Queen Elizabeth expressed "growing disbelief and total shock."

RUSSIA — Russia put troops on alert. President Vladimir V. Putin held an emergency meeting of security officials and said he supported a tough response to the "barbaric acts."

Chancellor Gerhard Schröder

GERMANY — Chancellor Gerhard Schröder described the attacks as "a declaration of war against the civilized world." Authorities urged Frankfurt, the country's financial capital, to close all its major skyscrapers. The new Jewish museum in Berlin canceled its public opening.

ASIA

President Jiang Zemin

CHINA — President Jiang Zemin said he was "shocked" and sent his condolences to President Bush, while the Foreign Ministry said China "opposed all manner" of terrorism.

AFGHANISTAN — Taliban officials rejected suggestions that Osama bin Laden, the Saudi militant whom they are sheltering, could be behind the attacks. Asked if the Taliban condemned them, Foreign Minister Wakil Ahmed Muttawakil said, "We have criticized and we are now again criticizing terrorism in all its forms."

Prime Minister Junichiro Koizumi

JAPAN — Prime Minister Junichiro Koizumi expressed "great anger" and said, "These acts of terrorism should not be forgiven." Special security precautions were ordered at all United States military installations.

THE AMERICAS

CANADA — Hundreds of United States-bound flights were diverted to Canadian airports, including a plane carrying President Glafcos Clerides of Cyprus, who landed in Montreal.

President Vicente Fox

MEXICO — Increased security caused enormous traffic jams at the United States border and officials said they were considering closing the entire border. President Vicente Fox expressed "solidarity and our most profound condolences."

CUBA — The government expressed its "pain" and "solidarity" with its longtime adversary and offered air and medical facilities to help. State television took the unusual step of interrupting normal programming to announce the United States "national tragedy" and show CNN's Spanish-language channel live.

MIDDLE EAST

Yasir Arafat

WEST BANK AND GAZA —
Yasir Arafat, the Palestinian leader, expressed shock at the attacks, and offered condolences and help in hunting the attackers if it was requested. Several militant Palestinian groups denied involvement, but celebratory gunfire echoed across the West Bank.

Prime Minister Ariel
Sharon

ISRAEL — Prime Minister Ariel Sharon declared a national day of mourning in solidarity with the United States and urged the world to fight terrorism.

IRAN — President Mohammad Khatami condemned "terrorist" attacks on the United States, which broke diplomatic ties with Iran after the 1979 Islamic revolution and has accused Iran of sponsoring terrorism.

IRAQ — State television hailed the attacks as the "operation of the century" which the United States deserved because of its "crimes against humanity." Iraq blames the United States and Britain for prolonging punitive United Nations sanctions imposed after Baghdad's 1990 invasion of Kuwait and retained after a United States-led coalition drove Iraqi troops from Kuwait in the 1991 gulf war.

AFRICA

Colonel Muammar
el-Qaddafi

LIBYA — Colonel Muammar el-Qaddafi condemned the "terrible" attacks on the United States and said his country was ready to send aid to the American people, the official JANA news agency reported.

NATO

At an emergency meeting of the alliance's ambassadors in Brussels, the secretary general, Lord Robertson, promised the United States that it could rely on its allies in North America and Europe for assistance and support, and pledged that those responsible would not get away with it.

UNITED NATIONS

Secretary General Kofi
Annan

Diplomats called for swift action by the Security Council to impose sanctions on any governments or groups found to be responsible. "We are all traumatized by this terrible tragedy," Secretary General Kofi Annan said. The headquarters building in New York was evacuated.

The collapse of the north tower, as seen from New Jersey.

5 a.m., September 12, 2001.

6 a.m., September 12, 2001.

II
SEPTEMBER 12–18, 2001

9.13.01   9.14.01   9.15.01

The Week After

Dan Barry

The Wednesday sun rose above an altered skyline to burn off any last hope that it had not been real: that we had not seen what we had seen, nor lost what we had lost. It was the 12th of September, and the beginning of another time.

In the months to come, the people of New York City would be praised for maintaining the confident stride of their great metropolis. But in that first week, theirs was not so much the march of resolve as it was the sleepwalk of grief. How could it be anything else, when a step in any direction brought another reminder: the red-rimmed eyes of strangers; the floral memorials sprouting outside fire stations; the fliers, thousands of them, bearing photographs of the missing and asking please, please, to call this number if you have any information. The slightest shift in the late-summer wind could summon the acrid scent of Lower Manhattan still burning.

There, on 16 ashen acres already being called the Pile, the Site, Ground Zero — a sacred burial ground — the awful finality was only just sinking in. Doctors with no one to treat stood idle, while soot-caked rescue workers returned from their shifts in hell with heads bowed, and the pervasive smell of flesh drove search dogs to distraction. When a Port Authority police officer was pulled from the rubble early on Wednesday, a throaty cheer went up for one returned to the fold of the living. He would be the last survivor, though; in the end, more than 2,800 had died.

Still, the firefighters and police officers and ironworkers frantically dug, around the clock and for many days afterward, driven by the maddening thoughts of what if: What if someone's father, someone's wife — my brother firefighter — lay breathing just beneath the next bucketful of debris? Grief and exhaustion conspired to play tricks with the mind: whispers and cellphone rings seemed to emanate from the dead ground.

The anguish was not confined to the site; it was on display in homes, in offices, on the streets. As Mayor Rudolph W. Giuliani walked down Greenwich Street one of those first days, a distraught woman emerged to beg him for help in finding her 44-year-old son. The mayor consoled her, assured her that the search for survivors was continuing unabated. She handed him her telephone number just in case, and as he walked away, the mother muttered to no one in particular: "My son is at the bottom of that pile."

Nor was the pain New York's alone. People from all over the world had died in one day's trinity of terror: the collapse of the World Trade Center, the piercing of the Pentagon and an airplane crash in rural Pennsylvania. And so, three days after the attacks, the world took pause. In Bhopal, schoolchildren clasped their hands in prayer. In London, people stood in silence after the noontime chimes of Big Ben. On the tiny Croation island of Lopud, at the edge of the Adriatic Sea, a national flag hung at half-staff. In Washington, President George W. Bush gathered with other leaders at the National Cathedral to remember the dead. "God bless America," he said, before heading north to pay

BUSH TELLS THE MILITARY TO 'GET READY'; BROADER SPY POWERS GAINING SUPPORT

9.16.01

NATION SHIFTS ITS FOCUS TO WALL STREET AS A MAJOR TEST OF ATTACK'S AFTERMATH

9.17.01

WALL ST. REOPENS SIX DAYS AFTER SHUTDOWN; STOCKS SLIDE 7%, BUT INVESTORS RESIST PANIC

9.18.01

respects at the place where two mighty towers of commerce had once loomed.

In the end, after all, New York had taken the brunt of the attacks; physically and psychically, the context of daily life had changed. Lunchtime bomb scares — at Grand Central Terminal, at LaGuardia Airport, in subway stations — sent thousands of people fleeing into the streets. The National Guard patrolled Penn Station, while a Coast Guard cutter sat anchored at the mouth of the Hudson River. Tourists vanished and residents nested, lending a ghostly feel to Manhattan streets not accustomed to quiet. A cabdriver explained the difference: he suddenly could not remember whether the Avenue of the Americas ran north or south.

Each passing day, though, brought slight movement toward a sorrowful acceptance of what had happened to the city. Small and defiant acts of resilience began to sprout, like crocuses cracking through a pavement of grief: the stock exchange reopened six days after the attack; the commuter trains resumed normal schedules; students returned to classes; and Broadway actors, trained to provoke thought about the human condition, led their audiences in singing "God Bless America."

All the while, lights brighter than Broadway's illuminated the choreography that had emerged from the chaos in Lower Manhattan. Volunteers handed out supplies and food to the weary would-be rescuers. Women lugging cases of bottled water turned hoarse while calling out, "Water! Water!" Ironworkers

slowly dismantled the skeletons of steel with the blossoming sparks of acetylene torches. The first truckloads of the estimated 1.2 billion tons of debris made their way to a landfill in Staten Island, to be scoured for photographs, jewelry, body parts — anything that might help to identify a victim. And every now and then, a city sanitation worker would appear — on Church Street, or Vesey, or Liberty — to push away the ashes with a broom.

But no level of efficiency could mask the horrific sadness of a singular crime that was too much with us, in the televised images, in the air, in the smoky plumes that rose from the funeral pyre. Some of it was ephemeral, of course, like the thousands of messages scrawled in the creamy dust of destruction that coated the windows and buildings surrounding ground zero. "Vernon Cherry Call Home," on Greenwich Street; "The Towers Will Rise Again," on Murray Street; "God Be With You Dana — Love, Mom," on West Broadway.

Those words would be washed away. But not the yawning absence of the towers and the people, so many people.

These days, when Norman Steinmetz of Staten Island takes the bus over the Verrazano-Narrows Bridge, he sits on the side facing the Atlantic Ocean, avoiding the majestic view of Lower Manhattan. He is 70 years old, a former New York City police officer, and he just cannot bear the altered view.

"Look at what happened to my beautiful city," he said, sobbing.

The Scene From Above

"There's no way an amateur could have, with any degree of reliability, done what was done yesterday," John Nance [an airline pilot, author and aviation analyst] said.

—**James Glanz**
SEPTEMBER 13, 2001

The threat of terrorism has always been, for most Americans, an abstraction. But that changed with Tuesday's spectacular televised attack. The toll went far beyond the thousands of lost lives and the destruction of the pre-eminent symbol of the New York skyline. Our sense of security and much of our innocence was lost as well.

—**Bob Herbert**
Op-Ed page
SEPTEMBER 13, 2001

A satellite view that includes Manhattan on September 12, 2001.

The dawn did not erase the preceding day's agony — no dawn could — and so New Yorkers ate their meals, did the dishes and put out the trash, the mundane tasks of life, but nothing felt the same. The city seemed ever so much more fragile and unfamiliar.

—N.R. KLEINFIELD
SEPTEMBER 13, 2001

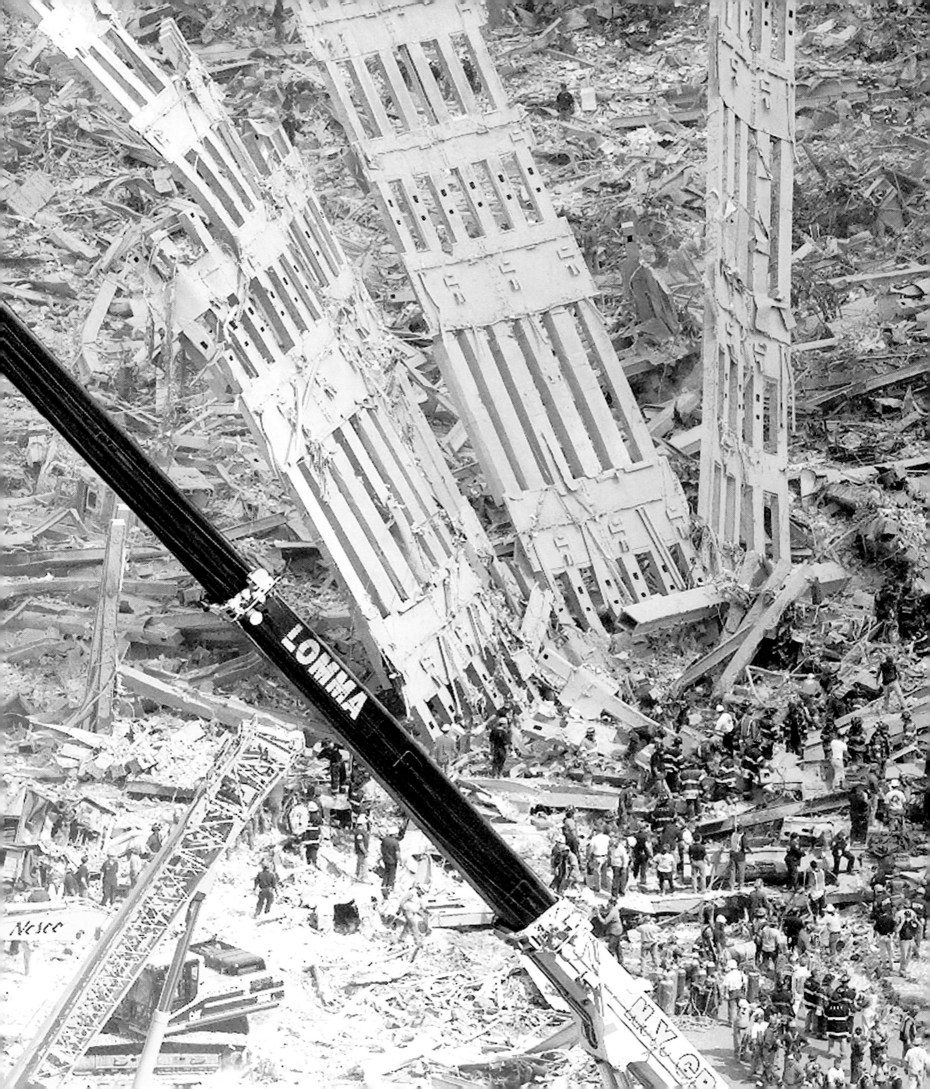

By late afternoon, the jaws of huge cranes were biting indiscriminately into the piles of rubble, while police officers, firefighters, soldiers and other rescue workers pried at the ground with shovels and crowbars.

—DAN BARRY
SEPTEMBER 13, 2001

Hundreds of emergency workers continue rescue efforts amid the wreckage of the World Trade Center.

RUTH FREMSON/NYT

A tea set in one of the apartments that faced 4 World Trade Center on Liberty Street.

SHARDS OF LIFE

For the thousands of people who live in Battery Park City, the past few days have been filled with anxiety, confusion and long waits for word that never seems to come on when they can go check on their homes.

Some people managed to get behind police lines and into their buildings long enough to gather clothes, money and other belongings. And by midday yesterday, people were allowed brief visits — "Not even 10 minutes," said [Cheryl] Morris [of Battery Park City] — to get their cats, dogs, hamsters and other pets.

But many others huddled at a staging area at Pier 40, at Houston and West Streets, turning it into an impromptu neighborhood gathering spot.

"Battery Park City is covered with debris and dust, much of which is granulated concrete, which in some places is three inches deep," James F. Gill, the chairman of the [Battery Park City] Authority, said in a statement.

Eventually, the residents will be allowed back, but many wondered yesterday whether they would stay in a place so close to the site of the worst terrorist attack in the United States.

A few said they would not stay, that the mass death was unbearable. "I do not want to live next to a graveyard," said Janey Fire, a museum photo services director who has lived in Battery Park City for less than a year.

But others remained undaunted, calculating that really, nowhere was completely safe.

Said Jeff Galloway, a lawyer who has lived in the complex for 20 years: "Where can you be in New York that is not close to some crazy person's target?"

—RANDAL C. ARCHIBOLD
SEPTEMBER 14, 2001

CHAPTER 2 - EXECUTION

A. DECLARATION OF A DISASTER:

In the event of a Disaster, which requires a declaration to Comdisco, only de[s] authorized staff may declare a Disaster. The Authorized Staff are members of the Dis[aster] Recovery Steering Committee and are fully cognizant of their responsibilities. A Disast[er] however, which affects the World Trade Center facility, may be declared by Port A[u]thority, th[e] General Manager and / or the Disaster Recovery Steering Committee depende[n]t upon the given situation. A declaration could be typically made on one of the following cas[es], but not necessarily limited to these:

1. A World Trade Center Disaster made be declared if the facility is rendered inopeable or the Port Authority so advises. The Group Head at the New Jersey Data Center is informed in order to prepare the Data Center.

2. In the case that the New Jersey Data Center has a Disaster, the General Manager is informed and the Disaster Recovery Steering Committee is convened, after assessing the situation, authorized staff will notify Comdisco and declare a Disaster.

3. A Disaster may also be declared due to technological failures, weather, and civil unrest or for any reason which renders the normal business operations inoperable.

4. Assessment of the Disaster levels will be made by the joint efforts of the Disaster Recovery Steering Committee. The judgment will be based upon the following factors:
   - The effects to the physical environment to the building.
   - Information from building security, Police / Fire
   - Effects on the normal business environment and the ability to continue operations

5. An evacuation will occur according to the procedures on the next page

A document found in Red Hook, Brooklyn. Comdisco, a disaster-recovery firm, had eight clients in the towers. Thousands of pages flew from the exploding towers and were carried by the wind to the western edge of Brooklyn, as well as to other areas of the city.

Today [Bush] said the attacks "were more than acts of terror; they were acts of war," a distinction intended to lay the military, political and psychological groundwork for military action.

—KATHARINE Q. SEELYE AND ELISABETH BUMILLER
SEPTEMBER 13, 2001

Members of the armed services stand guard along Chambers Street.

Mayor Rudolph W. Giuliani, center, leads Senator Charles Schumer of New York, second from left, Governor George E. Pataki of New York, second right, and Senator Hillary Rodham Clinton of New York, right, on a tour of the site. September 12, 2001.

POOL PHOTO BY ROBERT F. BUKATY

ANGEL FRANCO/NYT

National Guard checks the ID of a Wall Street worker. September 17, 2001.

THE MAYOR TAKES CHARGE

Mr. Giuliani was more than just a mayor. Day after day, his calm explanation of complicated, awful news helped to reassure a traumatized city that it would pull through, and that someone was in charge. He attended funerals, comforted survivors, urged residents to dine out and tourists to come in, all the while exuding compassion and resolve, even as the new threat of anthrax emerged. The man who had seemed so finished just a few weeks earlier was now being greeted with cheers wherever he went: Rudy! Rudy! Rudy!

— **DAN BARRY**
DECEMBER 31, 2001

President Bush, center, Mayor Rudolph W. Giuliani, left, Governor George E. Pataki, second from left, Senator Charles Schumer, second from right, and Fire Commissioner Thomas Van Essen, right, look toward the fallen buildings. September 14, 2001.

A New Leader Emerges

Sketching in the outline of an aggressive new American foreign policy, the Bush administration today gave the nations of the world a stark choice: stand with us against terrorism, deny safe havens to terrorists or face the certain prospect of death and destruction.

—**R.W. Apple Jr.**
SEPTEMBER 14, 2001

From left: President George W. Bush, First Lady Laura Bush, former President George Bush, Barbara Bush and former President Bill Clinton during a sermon recalling the terrorist attacks at a National Day of Prayer and Remembrance service at the National Cathedral in Washington, D.C. September 14, 2001.

Thousands of residents of Breezy Point, Queens, gathering on September 16 for a candlelight vigil to honor the casualties from their enclave in the attack on the World Trade Center. This community is home to many members of New York's police and fire departments.

An impromptu memorial at the Brooklyn Promenade with the skyline of Manhattan in the background. September 16, 2001.

A TIME TO MOURN

The city will survive because New York is too big and too ornery
to do anything else. But for the moment, this great city grieves.

—**BOB HERBERT**
Op-Ed page
SEPTEMBER 13, 2001

New York City: Scenes from vigils and memorial sites.

Taipei, Taiwan.

Nairobi, Kenya.

THE WORLD GRIEVES

T his week, "we are all New Yorkers."

—R.W. APPLE JR.
*quoting Dominique Moisu, French scholar
on international affairs*
SEPTEMBER 14, 2001

Southeastern University in Davie, Florida.

Los Angeles, California.

MONICA ALMEIDA/NYT

POOL PHOTO BY MAX NASH

Bhopal, India.

REUTERS

At Bellevue Hospital, a wall becomes a billboard for posters of some of the thousands of people still missing.

NANCY SIESEL/NYT

Engine Company 226 in Brooklyn Heights. Four of the five men who went out on September 11 never returned.

THE LOST BROTHERS

A total of 343 firefighters, nearly 30 times the number ever lost by the department in a single event, were killed in the attack. The dead included five of the department's most senior officials, including the chief who specialized in directing rescues from collapses of this sort. Also buried in the rubble: 91 fire trucks. The department pushed through promotions and accelerated hiring and, numerically, is back to full strength. But the loss of experience and the emotional hurt remain deeply felt throughout the ranks.

—**KEVIN FLYNN**

The firehouse on Eighth Avenue and 47th Street, known as the Pride of Midtown, is home to Engine Company 54, Ladder Company 4 and Battalion 9, which together lost 15 firefighters.

The Lost Firefighters

Joseph Agnello, Lad. 118 · Lt. Brian Ahearn, Bat. 13 · Eric Allen, Sqd. 18 · Richard Allen, Lad. 15 · Cpt. James Amato, Sqd. 1 · Calixto Anaya Jr., Eng. 4 · Joseph Angelini, Res. 1

Joseph Angelini Jr., Lad. 4 · Faustino Apostol Jr., Bat. 2 · David Arce, Eng. 33 · Louis Arena, Lad. 5 · Carl Asaro, Bat. 9 · Lt. Gregg Atlas, Eng. 10 · Gerald Atwood, Lad. 21

Gerard Baptiste, Lad. 9 · A.C. Gerard Barbara, Cmd. Ctr. · Matthew Barnes, Lad. 25 · Arthur Barry, Lad. 15 · Lt. Steven Bates, Eng. 235 · Carl Bedigian, Eng. 214 · Stephen Belson, Bat. 7

John Bergin, Res. 5 · Paul Beyer, Eng. 6 · Peter Bielfeld, Lad. 42 · Brian Bilcher, Sqd. 1 · Carl Bini, Res. 5 · Christopher Blackwell, Res. 3 · Michael Bocchino, Bat. 48 · Frank Bonomo, Eng. 230 · Gary Box, Sqd. 1 · Michael Boyle, Eng. 33 · Kevin Bracken, Eng. 40 · Michael Brennan, Lad. 4 · Peter Brennan, Res. 4

Cpt. Daniel Brethel, Lad. 24 · Cpt. Patrick Brown, Lad. 3 · Andrew Brunn, Lad. 5 · Cpt. Vincent Brunton, Lad. 105 · F.M. Ronald Bucca · Greg Buck, Eng. 201 · Cpt. William Burke Jr., Eng. 21 · A.C. Donald Burns, Cmd. Ctr. · John Burnside, Lad. 20 · Thomas Butler, Sqd. 1 · Patrick Byrne, Lad. 101 · George Cain, Lad. 7 · Salvatore Calabro, Lad. 101

Cpt. Frank Callahan, Lad. 35 · Michael Cammarata, Lad. 11 · Brian Cannizzaro, Lad. 101 · Dennis Carey, Hmc. 1 · Michael Carlo, Eng. 230 · Michael Carroll, Lad. 3 · Peter Carroll, Sqd. 1 · Thomas Casoria, Eng. 22 · Michael Cawley, Lad. 136 · Vernon Cherry, Lad. 118 · Nicholas Chiofalo, Eng. 235 · John Chipura, Eng. 219 · Michael Clarke, Lad. 2

Steven Coakley, Eng. 217 · Tarel Coleman, Sqd. 252 · John Collins, Lad. 25 · Robert Cordice, Sqd. 1 · Ruben Correa, Eng. 74 · James Coyle, Lad. 3 · Robert Crawford, Safety · Lt. John Crisci, H.M. · B.C. Dennis Cross, Bat. 57 · Thomas Cullen III, Sqd. 41 · Robert Curatolo, Lad. 16 · Lt. Edward D'Atri, Sqd. 1 · Michael D'Auria, Eng. 40

Scott Davidson, Lad. 118 · Edward Day, Lad. 11 · B.C. Thomas DeAngelis, Bat. 8 · Manuel Delvalle, Eng. 5 · Martin DeMeo, H.M. 1 · David DeRubbio, Eng. 226 · Lt. Andrew Desperito, Eng. 1 · B.C. Dennis Devlin, Bat. 9 · Gerard Dewan, Lad. 3 · George DiPasquale, Lad. 2 · Lt. Kevin Donnelly, Lad. 3 · Lt. Kevin Dowdell, Res. 4 · B.C. Raymond Downey, Soc.

Gerard Duffy, Lad. 21 · Cpt. Martin Egan Jr., Div. 15 · Michael Elferis, Eng. 22 · Francis Esposito, Eng. 235 · Lt. Michael Esposito, Sqd. 1 · Robert Evans, Eng. 33 · B.C. John Fanning, H.O. · Cpt. Thomas Farino, Eng. 26 · Terrence Farrell, Res. 4 · Cpt. Joseph Farrelly, Div. 1 · Dep. Comm. William Feehan · Lee Fehling, Eng. 235 · Alan Feinberg, Bat. 9

Michael Fiore, Res. 5 · Lt. John Fischer, Lad. 20 · Andre Fletcher, Res. 5 · John Florio, Eng. 214 · Lt. Michael Fodor, Lad. 21 · Thomas Foley, Res. 3 · David Fontana, Sqd. 1 · Robert Foti, Lad. 7 · Andrew Fredericks, Sqd. 18 · Lt. Peter Freund, Eng. 55 · Thomas Gambino Jr., Res. 3 · Chief of Dept. Peter Ganci Jr. · Lt. Charles Garbarini, Bat. 9

Thomas Gardner, Hmc. 1 · Matthew Garvey, Sqd. 1 · Bruce Gary, Eng. 40 · Gary Geidel, Res. 1 · B.C. Edward Geraghty, Bat. 9 · Denis Germain, Lad. 2 · Lt. Vincent Giammona, Lad. 5 · James Giberson, Lad. 35 · Ronnie Gies, Sqd. 288 · Paul Gill, Eng. 54 · Lt. John Ginley, Eng. 40 · Jeffrey Giordano, Lad. 3 · John Giordano, Hmc. 1

Keith Glascoe, Lad. 21 · James Gray, Lad. 20 · B.C. Joseph Grzelak, Bat. 48 · Jose Guadalupe, Eng. 54 · Lt. Geoffrey Guja, Bat. 43 · Lt. Joseph Gullickson, Lad. 101 · David Halderman, Sqd. 18 · Lt. Vincent Halloran, Lad. 8 · Robert Hamilton, Sqd. 41 · Sean Hanley, Lad. 20 · Thomas Hannafin, Lad. 5 · Dana Hannon, Eng. 26 · Daniel Harlin, Lad. 2

Lt. Harvey Harrell, Res. 5 · Lt. Stephen Harrell, Bat. 7 · Cpt. Thomas Haskell Jr., Div. 15 · Timothy Haskell, Sqd. 18 · Cpt. Terence Hatton, Res. 1 · Michael Haub, Lad. 4 · Lt. Michael Healey, Sqd. 41 · John Heffernan, Lad. 11 · Ronnie Henderson, Eng. 279 · Joseph Henry, Lad. 21 · William Henry, Res. 1 · Thomas Hetzel, Lad. 13 · Cpt. Brian Hickey, Res. 4

Lt. Timothy Higgins, S.O.C. · Jonathan Hohmann, Hmc. 1 · Thomas Holohan, Eng. 6 · Joseph Hunter, Sqd. 288 · Cpt. Walter Hynes, Lad. 13 · Jonathan Ielpi, Sqd. 288 · Cpt. Frederick Ill Jr., Lad. 2 · William Johnston, Eng. 6 · Andrew Jordan, Lad. 132 · Karl Joseph, Eng. 207 · Lt. Anthony Jovic, Bat. 47 · Angel Juarbe Jr., Lad. 12 · Mychal Judge, Chaplain

VINCENT KANE, ENG. 22 · B.C. CHARLES KASPER, S.O.C. · PAUL KEATING, LAD. 5 · RICHARD KELLY JR., LAD. 11 · THOMAS R. KELLY, LAD. 15 · THOMAS W. KELLY, LAD. 105 · THOMAS KENNEDY, LAD. 101 · LT. RONALD KERWIN, SQD. 288 · MICHAEL KIEFER, LAD. 132 · ROBERT KING JR., ENG. 33 · SCOTT KOPYTKO, LAD. 15 · WILLIAM KRUKOWSKI, LAD. 21 · KENNETH KUMPEL, LAD. 25

THOMAS KUVEIKIS, SQD. 252 · DAVID LAFORGE, LAD. 20 · WILLIAM LAKE, RES. 2 · ROBERT LANE, ENG. 55 · PETER LANGONE, SQD. 252 · SCOTT LARSEN, LAD. 15 · LT. JOSEPH LEAVEY, LAD. 15 · NEIL LEAVY, ENG. 217 · DANIEL LIBRETTI, RES. 2 · CARLOS LILLO, PARAMEDIC · ROBERT LINNANE, LAD. 20 · MICHAEL LYNCH, ENG. 40 · MICHAEL LYNCH, LAD. 4

MICHAEL LYONS, SQD. 41 · PATRICK LYONS, SQD. 252 · JOSEPH MAFFEO, LAD. 101 · WILLIAM MAHONEY, RES. 4 · JOSEPH MALONEY, LAD. 3 · B.C. JOSEPH MARCHBANKS JR., BAT. 12 · LT. CHARLES MARGIOTTA, BAT. 22 · KENNETH MARINO, RES. 1 · JOHN MARSHALL, ENG. 23 · LT. PETER MARTIN, RES. 2 · LT. PAUL MARTINI, ENG. 23 · JOSEPH MASCALI, T.S.U. 2 · KEITHROY MAYNARD, ENG. 33

BRIAN MCALEESE, ENG. 226 · JOHN MCAVOY, LAD. 3 · THOMAS MCCANN, BAT. 8 · LT. WILLIAM MCGINN, SQD. 18 · B.C. WILLIAM MCGOVERN, BAT. 2 · DENNIS MCHUGH, LAD. 13 · ROBERT MCMAHON, LAD. 20 · ROBERT MCPADDEN, ENG. 23 · TERENCE MCSHANE, LAD. 101 · TIMOTHY MCSWEENEY, LAD. 3 · MARTIN MCWILLIAMS, ENG. 22 · RAYMOND MEISENHEIMER, RES. 3 · CHARLES MENDEZ, LAD. 7

STEVE MERCADO, ENG. 40 · DOUGLAS MILLER, RES. 5 · HENRY MILLER JR., LAD. 105 · ROBERT MINARA, LAD. 25 · THOMAS MINGIONE, LAD. 132 · LT. PAUL MITCHELL, BAT. 1 · CAPT. LOUIS MODAFFERI, RES. 5 · LT. DENNIS MOJICA, RES. 1 · MANUEL MOJICA, SQD. 18 · CARL MOLINARO, LAD. 2 · MICHAEL MONTESI, RES. 1 · CAPT. THOMAS MOODY, DIV. 1 · B.C. JOHN MORAN, BAT. 49

VINCENT MORELLO, LAD. 35 · CHRISTOPHER MOZZILLO, ENG. 55 · RICHARD MULDOWNEY JR., LAD. 07 · MICHAEL MULLAN, LAD. 12 · DENNIS MULLIGAN, LAD. 2 · LT. RAYMOND MURPHY, LAD. 16 · LT. ROBERT NAGEL, ENG. 58 · JOHN NAPOLITANO, RES. 2 · PETER NELSON, RES. 4 · GERARD NEVINS, RES. 1 · DENNIS O'BERG, LAD. 105 · LT. DANIEL O'CALLAGHAN, LAD. 4 · DOUGLAS OELSCHLAGER, LAD. 15

JOSEPH OGREN, LAD. 3 · LT. THOMAS O'HAGAN, BAT. 4 · SAMUEL OITICE, LAD. 4 · PATRICK O'KEEFE, RES. 1 · CAPT. WILLIAM O'KEEFE, DIV. 15 · ERIC OLSEN, LAD. 15 · JEFFERY OLSEN, ENG. 10 · STEVEN OLSON, LAD. 3 · KEVIN O'ROURKE, RES. 2 · MICHAEL OTTEN, LAD. 35 · JEFFERY PALAZZO, RES. 5 · B.C. ORIO PALMER, BAT. 7 · FRANK PALOMBO, LAD. 105

PAUL PANSINI, ENG. 10 · B.C. JOHN PAOLILLO, BAT. 11 · JAMES PAPPAGEORGE, ENG. 23 · ROBERT PARRO, ENG. 8 · DURRELL PEARSALL, RES. 4 · LT. GLENN PERRY, BAT. 12 · LT. PHILIP PETTI, BAT. 7 · LT. KEVIN PFEIFER, ENG. 33 · LT. KENNETH PHELAN, BAT. 32 · CHRISTOPHER PICKFORD, ENG. 201 · SHAWN POWELL, ENG. 207 · VINCENT PRINCIOTTA, LAD. 7 · KEVIN PRIOR, SQD. 252

B.C. RICHARD PRUNTY, BAT. 2 · LINCOLN QUAPPE, RES. 2 · LT. MICHAEL QUILTY, LAD. 11 · RICARDO QUINN, PARAMEDIC · LEONARD RAGAGLIA, ENG. 54 · MICHAEL RAGUSA, ENG. 279 · EDWARD RALL, RES. 2 · ADAM RAND, SQD. 288 · DONALD REGAN, RES. 3 · LT. ROBERT REGAN, LAD. 118 · CHRISTIAN REGENHARD, LAD. 131 · KEVIN REILLY, ENG. 207 · LT. VERNON RICHARD, LAD. 7

JAMES RICHES, ENG. 4 · JOSEPH RIVELLI, LAD. 25 · MICHAEL ROBERTS, ENG. 214 · MICHAEL E. ROBERTS, LAD. 35 · ANTHONY RODRIGUEZ, ENG. 279 · MATTHEW ROGAN, LAD. 11 · NICHOLAS ROSSOMANDO, RES. 5 · PAUL RUBACK, LAD. 25 · STEPHEN RUSSELL, ENG. 55 · LT. MICHAEL RUSSO, S.O.C. · B.C. MATTHEW RYAN, BAT. 1 · THOMAS SABELLA, LAD. 13 · CHRISTOPHER SANTORA, ENG. 54

JOHN SANTORE, LAD. 5 · GREGORY SAUCEDO, LAD. 5 · DENNIS SCAUSO, H.M. 1 · JOHN SCHARDT, ENG. 201 · B.C. FRED SCHEFFOLD, BAT. 12 · THOMAS SCHOALES, ENG. 4 · GERARD SCHRANG, RES. 3 · GREGORY SIKORSKY, SQD. 41 · STEPHEN SILLER, SQD. 1 · STANLEY SMAGALA JR., ENG. 226 · KEVIN SMITH, H.M. 1 · LEON SMITH JR., LAD. 118 · ROBERT SPEAR JR., ENG. 26

JOSEPH SPOR, RES. 3 · B.C. LAWRENCE STACK, BAT. 50 · CPT. TIMOTHY STACKPOLE, DIV. 11 · GREGORY STAJK, LAD. 13 · JEFFERY STARK, ENG. 230 · BEMJAMIN SUAREZ, LAD. 21 · DANIEL SUHR, ENG. 216 · LT. CHRISTOPHER SULLIVAN, LAD. 111 · BRIAN SWEENEY, RES. 1 · SEAN TALLON, LAD. 10 · ALLAN TARASIEWICZ, RES. 5 · PAUL TEGTMEIER, ENG. 4 · JOHN TIERNEY, LAD. 9

JOHN TIPPING II, LAD. 4 · HECTOR TIRADO JR., ENG. 23 · RICHARD VANHINE, SQD. 41 · PETER VEGA, LAD. 118 · LAWRENCE VELING, ENG. 235 · JOHN VIGIANO II, LAD. 132 · SERGIO VILLANUEVA, LAD. 132 · LAWRENCE VIRGILIO, SQD. 18 · LT. ROBERT WALLACE, ENG. 205 · JEFFERY WALZ, LAD. 9 · LT. MICHAEL WARCHOLA, LAD. 5 (D) · CAPT. PATRICK WATERS, S.O.C. · KENNETH WATSON, ENG. 214

MICHAEL WEINBERG, ENG. 1 · DAVID WEISS, RES. 1 · TIMOTHY WELTY, SQD. 288 · EUGENE WHELAN, ENG. 230 · EDWARD WHITE, ENG. 230 · MARK WHITFORD, ENG. 23 · LT. GLENN WILKINSON, ENG. 238 · B.C. JOHN WILLIAMSON, BAT. 6 · CAPT. DAVID WOOLEY, LAD. 4 · RAYMOND YORK, ENG. 285

*A masked man fired 21 shots at Hassan Awday on September 12 as Mr. Awday, a Yemeni
American, stood behind a bulletproof-glass window at his gasoline station in Gary, Indiana.*

MISPLACED ANGER

"It is un-Islamic to kill innocent people," said a 25-year-old
Afghan police constable, Muhammad Anwar.

— **BARRY BEARAK**
SEPTEMBER 13, 2001

[A]s a Sikh man was trying to flee Lower Manhattan on Tuesday,
he found himself running not only from flames, but also from a
trio of men yelling invective about his turban.

— **SOMINI SENGUPTA**
SEPTEMBER 13, 2001

VOICES FROM A BROOKLYN MOSQUE

MOHAMMED AYESH: *"I work for a car service. When people get in, some — only a few — look at me with anger because of what happened. I don't blame them. Every human being falls into the same thing. They might have had relatives in the towers. But sometimes I blame them because it's not justified. Maybe I don't look like a white boy, but this tragedy hurt me, too."*

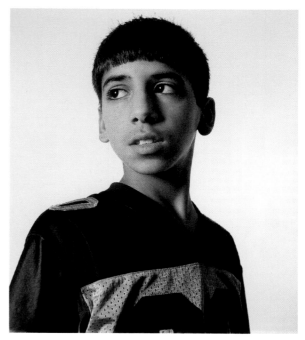

MOHAMMED QUNBAR: *"I'm 12. We saw the smoke from our school in Brooklyn. Later, we caught some papers that had been burnt. I was a little afraid someone might bomb our area. I think we might go to war. Why? Because Bush said so. But I don't think that's a good idea. War is not like one attack; it's a big deal. I feel frustrated and sad, but we can't do anything about it. It's done."*

SHEIKH MOHAMED MOUSSA IMAM: *"I'm the religious leader of the Muslim community here in Bay Ridge. The Koran says, 'Whoever slays a soul, unless it be for manslaughter or for mischief in the land, it is as though he slew all men.' What happened happened to us as well. We are all fellow Americans. A lot of people have come here in the past few days to share their grief."*

JOSHEPH THALAM: *"I came to New York from Jordan in April. Since the attack, I have been sad. Those people died for no reason. If I was a police officer, I would shoot their fathers and family. I hope the U.S. government will attack those terrorists and kill them in their homes. What they did was for the devil. It will never happen again. Next time, American pilots will attack them."*

PHOTOGRAPHS BY ANDRES SERRANO FOR NYT
INTERVIEWS BY CATHERINE SAINT LOUIS
PUBLISHED ON SEPTEMBER 23, 2001

New York Stock Exchange reopens.
September 17, 2001.

BARTON SILVERMAN/NYT

The Mosque Foundation in Bridgeview,
Illinois. September 13, 2001.

JOHN ZICH/AGENCE FRANCE-PRESSE

At the Lincoln Tunnel in Weehawken,
New Jersey. September 13, 2001.

KEITH MEYERS/NYT

A couple watches fighter jets from their window
in Manhattan. September 14, 2001.

TING-LI WANG/NYT

An old pier next to the Imperial Water Ferry in Hoboken, New Jersey. September 13, 2001.

PHOTOGRAPHS BY BILL CUNNINGHAM/NYT

On day three at the World Trade Center site, firefighters and other rescue workers labor around the clock. September 13, 2001.

September 15, 2001.

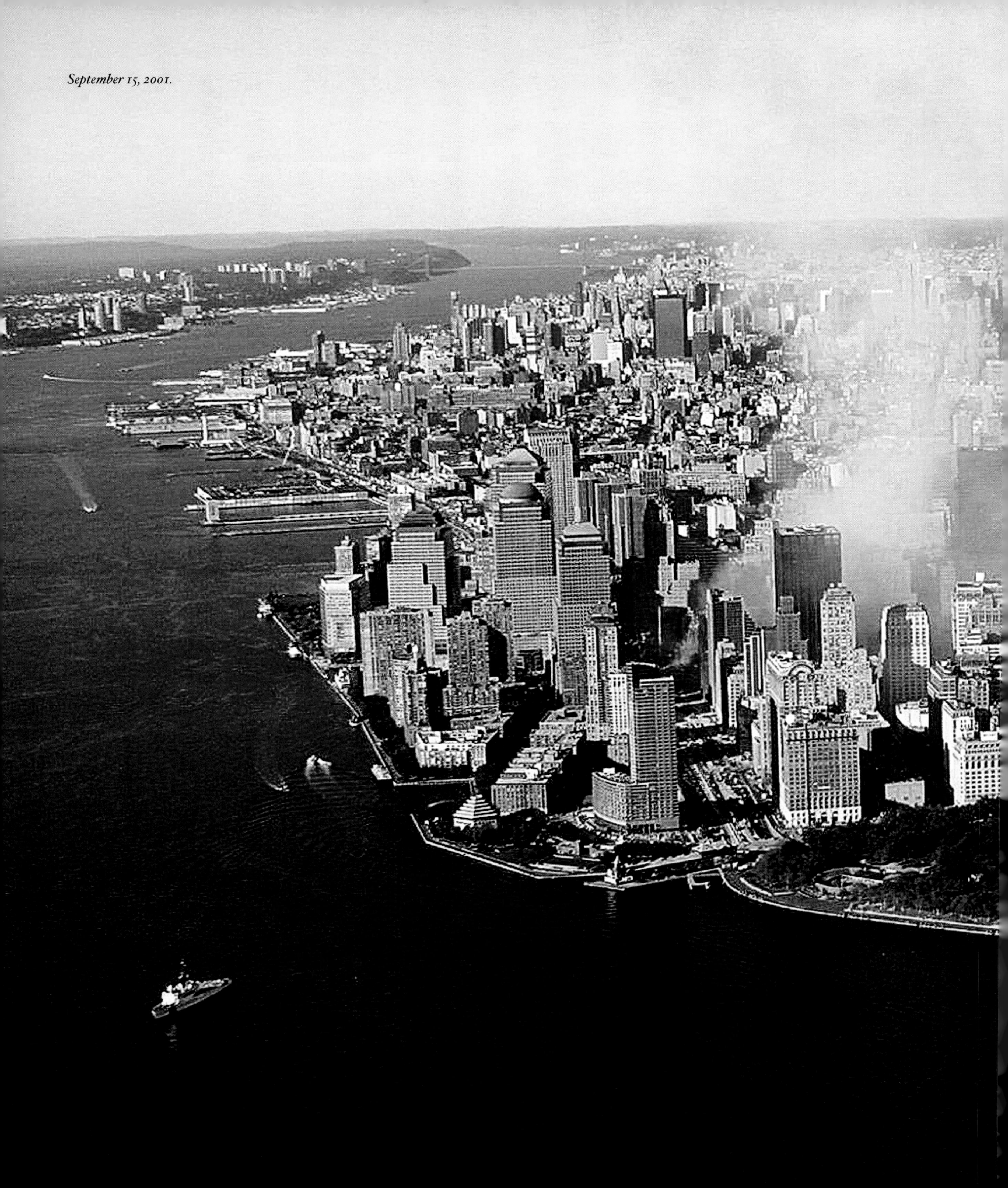

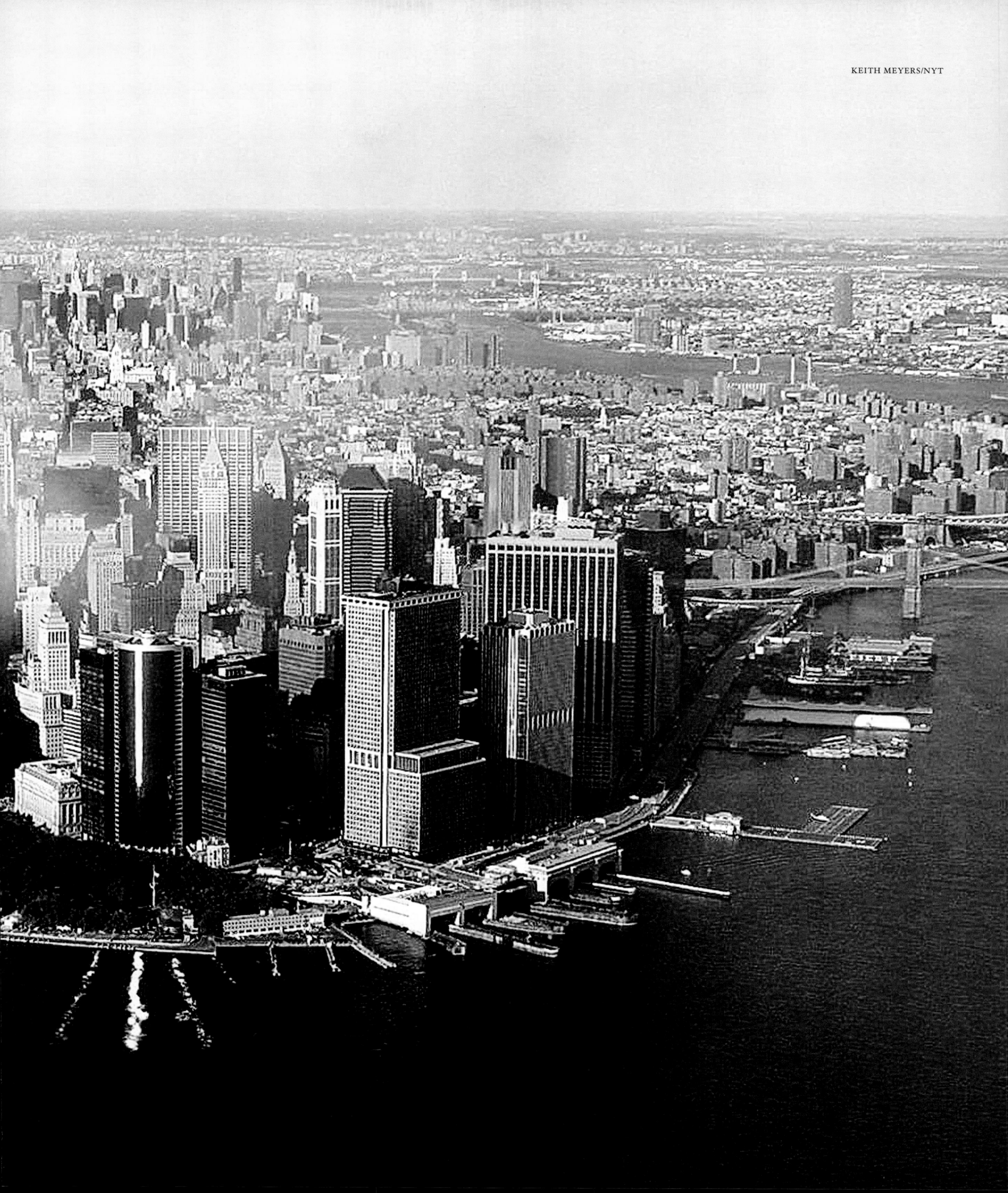

KEITH MEYERS/NYT

September 13, 2001.

EDWARD KEATING/NYT

III

THE CHALLENGE AT HOME

Aftermath in America

Celestine Bohlen

By October 11, one month after the attacks, the nation had managed to catch its breath and collect its strength, although that did little to diminish the pain, or even the fear. It would be another month before United States forces and their Afghan allies flushed the Taliban out of Kabul. But in those first weeks of war, the images of high-flying bombers emblazoned with emblems of the New York City Fire Department, laying waste to Al Qaeda training camps, gave Americans the sense that justice was being served.

"We have entered a struggle of uncertain duration," said President George W. Bush at a commemoration ceremony on that day, "but we can be certain of the outcome."

By March 11, the six-month anniversary, an American victory in Afghanistan seemed virtually certain after a fierce ground battle in the Shah-i-Kot valley. By this time, the United States had signaled its determination to take its war on terrorism to other parts of the world, stepping up pressure on the "axis of evil," in Mr. Bush's phrase. But as the administration expanded its list of potential targets, with Iraq at the top of the list, it was finding that its allies were not so eager to support a war whose terms were increasingly dictated by Washington alone.

Mr. Bush first called the country to arms on September 20, when he spoke to a joint session of Congress. "Our grief has turned to anger and anger to resolution," he said in a widely praised speech. The president's stature clearly grew after that and so did his ratings. According to a New York Times/CBS poll published in late October, 87 percent of those interviewed approved of his handling of the job.

His standing was buoyed by an extraordinary outburst of patriotism that soon had the whole country waving flags: the Stars and Stripes appeared on cars, trains, buses, front porches

Wall Street on September 17, 2001 — the day the New York Stock Exchange reopened.

and store windows everywhere. Few challenged the national leadership at a time of crisis, and one late-night television talk show host who questioned the notion that the airplane hijackers were "cowards" was shunned by sponsors, and rebuked by the White House spokesman.

Leading a shaken country into a war against an elusive enemy required extraordinary measures, and the Bush administration did not hesitate to take them. On October 25, both the House of Representatives and the Senate voted overwhelmingly to grant the government sweeping new powers to hunt down suspected terrorists. Those included broader authority to detain immigrants without charge, penetrate money-laundering banks, conduct wiretaps and seek out information stored on the computers of possible terrorists. "We treat terrorism with kid gloves in the current criminal code," said Senator Orrin G. Hatch of Utah. "This bill stops that."

National security became the watchword. Guards appeared at the entrances of office buildings, Broadway theaters and the Liberty Bell in Philadelphia, checking identification, opening handbags. A small but extremely scary outbreak of anthrax cases — the work of an unknown bioterrorist — increased the national level of nervousness and exposed the vulnerability of such well-guarded institutions as the United States Congress. Even the Capitol was shut down temporarily. By October 16, the F.B.I. had received 2,300 reports of suspicious white powder. And that was not the only new source of worry. Three times in three months, Washington issued warnings of possible new terrorist attacks, although no details were made available. Even Tom Ridge, the newly named head of Homeland Security, admitted that it was difficult to stay alert and return to normal — at the same time. "It's a difficult and fine line that we walk," he said.

But national habits did change: for months, the nation was gripped by a fear of flying, costing the airlines an estimated $7 billion and crippling the tourist industry. Passengers did slowly return to the airports, encouraged perhaps by legislation passed by Congress that turned 28,000 airport security personnel into full-fledged federal employees, for at least three years. Until then, airport security had been the responsibility of the airlines, which had relied on undertrained, underpaid workers — often immigrants who rarely stayed long in their jobs.

As an investigation into the September 11 hijackers continued across several continents, a full-scale assault was launched on the financial networks that had backed them, and sanctions were imposed on 22 organizations that had links to Al Qaeda, including Hamas and Hezbollah abroad; at home Islamic charities that were accused of funneling money to the terrorists were shut down. By the late fall, more than 1,000 people had been arrested and detained, although neither their names nor the charges against them were made public.

Henry Boyle, 13, put flowers on the bombed-out cars in his neighborhood. September 12, 2001.

brought to a United States base in Cuba.

The months after September 11 were also a time to take stock and assess the damage. In the first weeks, the death toll at the World Trade Center and the Pentagon soared beyond 5,000. By April 22, seven months after the attacks, the number had dropped to 2,825.

But even in March, bodies of victims were still being found at ground zero as 7,000 workers continued to sift through tons of awful rubble, working night and day, several days a week in all kinds of weather. The site itself had burned for months, haunting lower Manhattan with fine gray dust and a cloying stench. But the stream of visitors who came to look, with awe, at the scale of the destruction confirmed what relatives already knew: this was, and will always be, hallowed ground.

There were other ways to count the losses. Economically, the country had taken an enormous hit that was delivered just as a recession was gathering strength. An initial report put the economic impact of September 11 on New York City alone at a staggering $105 billion. By October, the city had lost 79,000 jobs, while nationally the unemployment rate climbed to 5.4 percent.

In the heightened anxiety, some began to worry out loud that the headlong rush to improve national security was coming at the expense of civil liberties. Congress, for instance, balked at an administration proposal to detain immigrants under suspicion indefinitely. The final bill set a seven-day limit on the detentions, which could be and often were extended to six months under certain circumstances. There was fresh outrage later over a Justice Department order that authorized eavesdropping on communications between lawyers and federal prisoners and over a presidential order (later modified in some respects) that allowed foreigners charged with terrorism to be tried by military tribunals, a legal mechanism that had not been used in the United States since World War II. Foreign governments openly protested the United States' refusal to give prisoner of war status to Taliban and Al Qaeda fighters

By spring, the national economy seemed poised for a recovery and some dire predictions like a drop in the New York real estate market never did come true. And as the war against terrorism moved to its new and broader phase, President Bush made an effort in a speech before the Washington diplomatic corps to acknowledge that Americans were not the only ones who had suffered at the hands of terrorists, and not the only ones who were dying in the fight to defeat them. In pledging a global commitment to the struggle, he said the United States would provide military aid to "governments everywhere." "Our coalition must act deliberately," he declared, "but inaction is not an option."

Clouds of smoke make the work even more difficult at ground zero on October 11, 2001. Some 300 firefighters exposed to smoke and dust from the disaster were on leave for respiratory problems, as of January 2002.

A ramp atop the subterranean remains of the World Trade Center's north tower lets heavy equipment travel far below ground to remove debris. Water is slowly accumulating in the deepest parts of the pit. January 11, 2002.

UNDER GROUND ZERO

Now, the army of laborers — along with teams of firefighters still diligently looking for human remains — have moved below ground, sinking floor by floor into the subterranean realm of an office complex that, even in the horrific implosion of the towers, somehow was not smashed flat.

Like archaeologists digging among ancient ruins, they must exhaustingly think out each step. The unlighted, below-ground floors and the scattered structures in whose shadow the crews labor are not just the last vestiges of an office complex. They are also buttressing an adjacent wall — known colloquially as the bathtub, or slurry wall — that surrounds much of the site and keeps back the waters of the Hudson River.

To date, according to the city's count, 1,036,837 tons of charred steel, smashed concrete, crumpled ductwork and other assorted debris have been removed from the site since September 11.

So compressed are the piles of remaining debris in the footprint of the north tower that as the backhoes and grapplers reach for pieces of twisted steel, they must struggle again and again to yank them free. The rear ends of these massive vehicles are lifted precariously into the air as they pull at the buried debris, and they rock back and forth like children's toys.

— ERIC LIPTON AND JAMES GLANZ
JANUARY 13, 2002

The Site

*The excavation effort at the World Trade Center site is making
its way down to the deepest parts of the seven-story basement.*

The U.S. Customs House, 6 W.T.C., was destroyed by falling debris.

NORTH ➡

WEST ST. LIBERTY ST. **2 W.T.C.** (Approx.) **1 W.T.C.** (Approx.) Partly intact basement slabs VERIZON BUILDING **7 W.T.C.** (Approx.)

SUBWAY ① ⑨

SOUTH END OF BATHTUB WALL

Bundles of steel cable, known as tiebacks, continue to be installed through the bathtub wall into the bedrock to hold back the Hudson River.

BATHTUB WALL

TIEBACK

BEDROCK

Rain water and seepage

Partly excavated former shopping area

VESEY ST.

THE NEW YORK TIMES

November 22, 2001.

BRAD LAPAYNE

January 5, 2002.

THE CHALLENGE AT HOME

March 14, 2002.

THE CHALLENGE AT HOME

AFTERSHOCKS BELOW

The scene underneath 5 World Trade Center, 10 days after the attack. Two patrol members search for signs of looting at Sbarro's Pizzeria and other underground shops. September 21, 2001.

The devastation above ground at the World Trade Center site is obvious to anyone with a television set. But below the street, in spaces that are home to much of what keeps New York City running, billions of dollars of damage remains unseen.

The costs of rebuilding underground will be amplified compared with the work being done above ground because of the density of items below Lower Manhattan. It is the most crowded underbelly in the world, with hundreds of miles of wires, pipes, tunnels and cables.

—JAYSON BLAIR
OCTOBER 14, 2001

SUBWAY DAMAGE

Beneath the World Trade Center rubble, New York City Transit has sealed off 1,800 feet of the damaged 1 and 9 subway line between two concrete walls. The methods for stabilizing the road overlying a damaged section are shown below.

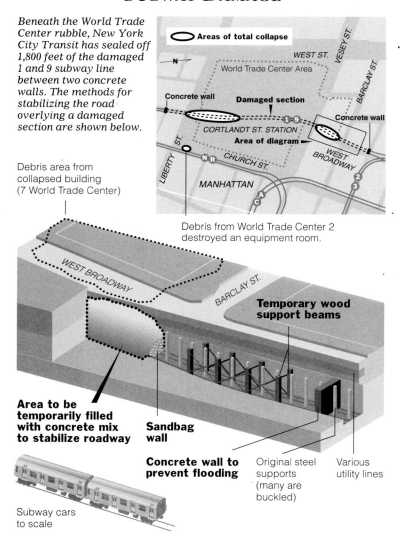

Source: Metropolitan Transportation Authority—New York City Transit

THE NEW YORK TIMES

A team of New York City Transit engineers and contractors went underground, past the abandoned turnstiles and token booths of the Cortlandt Street station that served the trade center. It was a journey, one engineer said, that felt like a visit to the Titanic.

Wearing respirators and hard hats, equipped with flashlights and gas meters to detect any chemicals lingering in the air, the team lumbered along the station's platform toward a truly hellish sight. A chunk of the south tower had tumbled down, dozens of stories, to a final stop right there in the gloom of the tunnel.

The subway tunnel floor, ceiling and walls must be rebuilt, new track installed, the signal and communications system replaced, all somehow by November or December, when the line is set to reopen.

—ERIC LIPTON AND JAMES GLANZ
JANUARY 13, 2002

Engineers tested the integrity of the Cortlandt Street subway station to determine whether it is structurally sound and what is required to restore service. New York City Transit officials have determined that the damage is so extensive that more than one mile of line will have to be rebuilt. September 28, 2001.

Workers carry buckets of debris out of the site on September 24, 2001.

SEARCHING THE DEBRIS

When the bodies are gone, the work resumes and all the undramatic things familiar only to the ground zero crew assume their proper places. The excavators claw through the pile. The ironworkers are hoisted in a bucket to burn away the remaining wall. It rains fire, pressurized water dissipates into mist and the blowtorches produce an eerie green vapor. The pit fumes a white stinking smoke. Men shout. The falling metal makes the sound of the ocean booming as it breaks over the shore. The smells are of burning wiring, dankness from the subway tunnels and the sweet, acrid cherrylike smell of death.

—**CHARLIE LeDuff**
SEPTEMBER 24, 2001

Workers cut steel, so it can be hauled away from the disaster site. October 20, 2001.

EDWARD KEATING/NYT

THE COLLAPSE

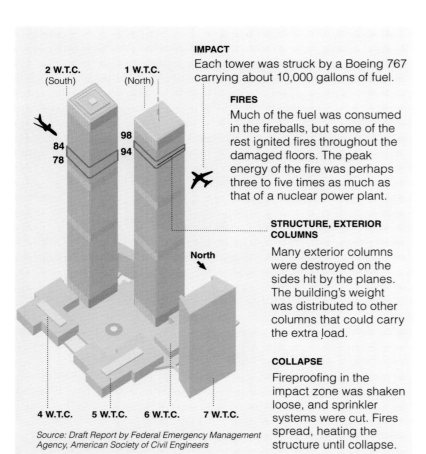

2 W.T.C. (South)   **1 W.T.C.** (North)

98
84
94
78

North

4 W.T.C.   5 W.T.C.   6 W.T.C.   7 W.T.C.

Source: Draft Report by Federal Emergency Management Agency, American Society of Civil Engineers

IMPACT
Each tower was struck by a Boeing 767 carrying about 10,000 gallons of fuel.

FIRES
Much of the fuel was consumed in the fireballs, but some of the rest ignited fires throughout the damaged floors. The peak energy of the fire was perhaps three to five times as much as that of a nuclear power plant.

STRUCTURE, EXTERIOR COLUMNS
Many exterior columns were destroyed on the sides hit by the planes. The building's weight was distributed to other columns that could carry the extra load.

COLLAPSE
Fireproofing in the impact zone was shaken loose, and sprinkler systems were cut. Fires spread, heating the structure until collapse.

THE NEW YORK TIMES; ILLUSTRATION BY JOHN PAPASIAN

Fireproofing, sprinkler systems and the water supply for hoses were all disabled in the twin towers on September 11 in the face of a blaze so intense that it drove temperatures as high as 2,000 degrees and generated heat equivalent to the energy output of a nuclear power plant, a federal report on how the towers fell has concluded.

The report, a copy of which was obtained by The New York Times, provides documentary evidence that simultaneously supports and rejects many of the theories about what happened to the towers on September 11.

Under normal circumstances, fire suppression systems are designed to allow a high-rise blaze to burn itself out before the building collapses. But the report concludes that there were across-the-board failures in the towers' fire suppression systems, raising disturbing questions about the safety and integrity of other tall buildings in out-of-control fires. But the ultimate significance of those failures is extremely difficult to gauge, the report says, because of the extraordinary circumstances of the attack.

The draft report also does not contain any discussion of what could become a contentious new issue in attempts to explain why the south tower, though struck after the north tower, fell first. That question involves a program, started after the 1993 bombing of the towers, to increase the thickness of the fireproofing on the lightweight steel joists that held up the floors.

The report cites the tight clustering of the exit stairways, three per tower, as a factor that may have made it easier to cause damage to all of them with one blow. These exit stairwells also had relatively lightweight gypsum board sheathing, providing little armor. Partly for these reasons, thousands of people above the floors of impact were trapped.

Most of the tenants in the floors below impact, to the credit of the building and the emergency lighting in the stairwells, escaped.

—**JAMES GLANZ AND ERIC LIPTON**
MARCH 29, 2002

South Tower

IMPACT 9:02:54 a.m. **COLLAPSE** 9:59:04 a.m.

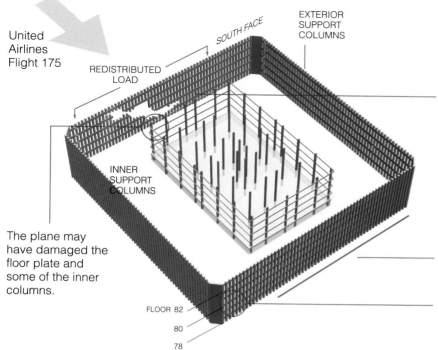

United Airlines Flight 175

REDISTRIBUTED LOAD

SOUTH FACE

EXTERIOR SUPPORT COLUMNS

INNER SUPPORT COLUMNS

The plane may have damaged the floor plate and some of the inner columns.

FLOOR 82
80
78

Weight supported by the destroyed exterior columns was redistributed to adjacent ones. It is believed that the additional weight was within the columns' load capacity. Initially, floors near the impact suffered severe damage across a horizontal span of about 70 feet.

The impact is believed to have disrupted the sprinkler and fire standpipe systems, preventing operation. However, even if these systems had not been damaged, they probably would have been ineffective. The initial flash fire would have activated so many sprinklers that the system would have quickly depressurized. Also, the fire was so extensive that sprinklers would have done little good.

Most intense fires.

A stream of molten material — thought to be aluminum from the plane — flowed down the side of the building.

North Tower

IMPACT 8:46:26 a.m. **COLLAPSE** 10:28:31 a.m.

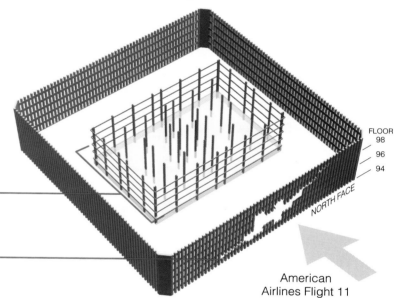

FLOOR 98
96
94

NORTH FACE

American Airlines Flight 11

As the plane plowed through the building, it created a cloud of jet fuel that ignited into fireballs, burning an estimated 1,000 to 3,000 gallons of jet fuel. The resulting pressure was sufficient to break windows, but not enough to cause significant structural damage.

People on the 91st floor described extensive debris in this area of the building, suggesting that some sections of the floors above may have collapsed.

Floors supported by the missing sections of exterior walls appear to have partly collapsed across a horizontal span of about 65 feet.

The Impacts

Some parts of the planes went completely through the buildings and landed as far as six blocks away. Life jackets and parts of seats were found on the roof of a nearby building.

SOUTH TOWER   NORTH TOWER

VESEY ST.
6 WTC   5 WTC
WEST ST.   1 WTC NORTH TOWER   CHURCH ST.
2 WTC SOUTH TOWER   4 WTC
LIBERTY ST.

FIREBALLS

LANDING GEAR

FUSELAGE SECTION

LANDING GEAR

WHEEL

NORTH

The Collapses

SOUTH TOWER

1. Partial collapse of floor in the southeast corner.

2. Collapse of entire floor along the east side with columns along the east face buckling near the floor, from south to north.

3. Top of the building twists to the east and south, and collapses.

NORTH TOWER

1. Television antenna begins to fall, suggesting failure of inner columns.

2. The portion of the building above the impact fell as a unit, pushing down a cushion of air.

3. The air fed fires in the impact area, creating the illusion of an explosion.

EXTERIOR STEEL COLUMNS

HEAVY DEBRIS, EXTERIOR STEEL COLUMNS

LIGHT DEBRIS, ALUMINUM CLADDING

Circles mark areas where parts of the building fell.

Source: Draft report by the Federal Emergency Management Agency and American Society of Civil Engineers

BADEN COPELAND, MIKA GRÖNDAHL, WILLIAM MCNULTY, SARAH SLOBIN AND ARCHIE TSE/NYT

PHOTOGRAPHS BY FRED R. CONRAD/NYT

*After an initial sifting process, debris from the World Trade Center is spread over
an open field at the Fresh Kills landfill. Detectives rake through it and pull out
personal items, like scraps of clothing. October 19, 2001.*

*ID and credit cards (above) and watches (right) are among the many
items that have been recovered at Fresh Kills Landfill and will be
returned to their owners or their families. January 14, 2002.*

A worker in protective gear with his equipment — pitchforks and shovels — at Fresh Kills landfill. October 10, 2001.

GRIM TASK

It is something that has never been done. Without precedent to guide them, through trial and error, the Police Department and various other government agencies have developed a fairly sophisticated process to refine crudely jumbled debris. On a 135-acre, waste-made plateau rising 180 feet in central Staten Island — where there had been nothing but a foul wind and a glorious view — they have built a village to sort the evidence of a singular crime.

Three hundred thousand tons of rubble — about one-quarter of the disaster's total — have been taken by barge and truck to the landfill. There, as many as 300 detectives at a time, working 12-hour shifts, have pored over nearly two-thirds of that amount.

To date, they have found more than 1,700 body parts and about 1,600 items — from jewelry to credit cards to a set of keys — that might lead to the identification of one of the thousands of people listed as missing.

Many [items], like rings and wristwatches, that will not neccesarily help with identifications will be saved nonetheless; they may have enormous value for families left with little else. The department plans to catalog the items so they can be identified and returned to families efficiently and compassionately.

— **DAN BARRY AND AMY WALDMAN**
OCTOBER 21, 2001

New York is a city of increasing heartbreak, with no
respite in sight. "It is absolutely worse than you could
ever imagine," said Rudy Weindler [a firefighter who
spent 12 mostly fruitless hours looking for survivors in
the smoke and the debris].

BOB HERBERT
Op-Ed page
SEPTEMBER 13, 2001

A firefighter pulled from the wreckage on January 1, 2002.

A FINAL TRIBUTE

Debris from the World Trade Center was placed into thousands of urns for the victims' families.

CHESTER HIGGINS JR./NYT

In a process invested with solemn ceremony, [police] officers [filled] at least 4,000 small round urns of polished cherry mahogany with powdered debris from the World Trade Center attack. The urns [were] given to the victims' families at a memorial service at the end of October.

Three 55-gallon drums were filled and blessed by a chaplain at ground zero, then taken by police escort to One Police Plaza. There, they were blessed again, and placed in a narrow, newly cleaned and painted room. The drums are covered with American flags. They are flanked by two honor guards, forward gazes unwavering, who stand sentry 24 hours a day.

The soil is scooped from the drums into a wooden box, resembling a small coffin, that the department constructed for this purpose alone. The box is taken to an adjacent door, and placed on one of the black-clad tables.

An officer scoops a large spoonful of soil into a plastic bag. The soil, brown with a slightly grayish cast, is unhealthy in appearance. It crunches slightly when the spoon is placed in it, and it is thick enough that the spoon stands on its own.

Another officer folds the plastic bag in half, then closes it with a red tie and places it in the five-inch-high urn, with 09-11-01 etched on the side. A white-gloved officer carries the urn to another table, where officers use power drivers to seal it with two brass Phillips screws. Gloved hands convey the urn to yet another table, where it is carefully inspected, then placed in a white cloth bag for safekeeping.

Each urn [was] presented in a blue velvet bag inside a black box. A family may choose to affix an engraved nameplate to its flat top.

—**AMY WALDMAN**
OCTOBER 15, 2001

RICHARD PERRY/NYT

Fragment of steel was lifted from the rubble into an upright position.

In Memoriam

Funeral of an EMS worker at Mount Hope Cemetery. September 14, 2001.

Firefighters give a blessing at the funeral for Mychal F. Judge, the Franciscan Friar who was Chaplain of the Fire Department of New York City. September 15, 2001.

Funeral for New York City Fire Captain Terence Hatton at St. Patrick's Cathedral. October 4, 2001.

RICHARD PERRY/NYT

A funeral for members of the F.D.N.Y. at St. Patrick's Cathedral in New York City. November 5, 2001.

JUSTIN LANE FOR NYT

Above and right: About 10,000 people showed up at Madison Square Garden for a job fair on October 26, 2001.

New Jobless

The terrorists who attacked the World Trade Center may have been trying to crush American capitalism and its masters of the universe on Wall Street. But the economic impact of the attack is felling a very different group of people: cooks, cabdrivers, sales clerks and seamstresses.

Workers in traditionally low-wage industries, like restaurants and hotels, retailing and transportation, have been hit hard in the fallout from September 11, according to a new analysis from the New York State Department of Labor.

And a report released yesterday by the labor-backed Fiscal Policy Institute forecasts that almost 80,000 people will have lost their jobs by the end of the year and that 60 percent of these positions paid an average of $23,000 a year. That is far below the citywide average salary of roughly $58,000.

— **Leslie Eaton and Edward Wyatt**
November 6, 2001

Unemployed After the Attack

Top 10 occupations most affected by the events of September 11.

OCCUPATION	ESTIMATED LAYOFFS	AVERAGE HOURLY WAGE
Waiters and waitresses	4,225	$7.08
Cleaning and maintenance workers	3,365	14.90
Sales representatives (retail)	2,843	9.15
Food preparation workers	2,284	8.90
Cashiers	2,282	7.36
Housekeeping workers	1,840	13.42
Food preparation and fast-food servers	1,718	7.09
General managers and top executives	1,367	51.34
Sales supervisors	1,183	22.42
Service supervisors	1,070	16.46

Source: Fiscal Policy Institute   THE NEW YORK TIMES

THE ANTHRAX PANIC

The fires were still raging at ground zero — and a frantic search for any survivors was under way — when public health officials in New York City sent out an urgent alert. The terrorist strike might not be over, the city warned hundreds of doctors and emergency rooms. An attack with anthrax spores, botulism, smallpox, even the plague, might well be next.

That warning — sent out before dawn on September 12 — turned out to be disturbingly prescient: the largest bioterrorism attack in United States history was about to begin. And before it would mysteriously peter out nearly three months later, five people would be dead and another 18 would have or be suspected of having anthrax.

But despite the early warning in New York and other precautionary alerts by federal officials, the anthrax attack went undetected for nearly a month, as people fell ill but their illness was not immediately identified. When the news finally did erupt — first in Florida, then in New York, then in Washington and New Jersey and finally Connecticut — intense nervousness, bordering on panic, swept the nation. To make matters worse, federal officials, including scientists, simply confessed ignorance about how widespread and lethal the threat might be or who was responsible.

Fears escalated as poisoned letters suddenly started turning up, one after another, at the NBC News office in Rockefeller Center in New York, at the Capitol Hill office of Senator Tom Daschle of South Dakota, at the New York Post headquarters in Manhattan. The United States Capitol closed down. New York's governor shut his New York City office. Thousands of reports about suspicious packages flooded police stations around the country; even the crumbs from powdered doughnuts inspired 911 calls. Demand surged for antibiotics and some pharmacies ran out of the most effective anthrax treatment.

Ultimately, only four poisoned letters were found and evidence was found suggesting that at least three others had been sent. The anthrax-spiked letters contained cryptic warnings that seemed to tie them clearly to the World Trade Center and Pentagon attacks: "09-11-01. YOU CAN NOT STOP US. WE HAVE THIS ANTHRAX. YOU DIE NOW. ARE YOU AFRAID?" read the letter sent to Senator Daschle, which had

been postmarked in Trenton, New Jersey, on September 18. But what did it mean? Were foreign terrorists launching a second strike? Or were the references to September 11 — even the words in one poisoned letter, "ALLAH IS GREAT" — merely decoys by a domestic group of terrorists or an isolated, angry American trying to exploit the lingering horror of the attack on the World Trade Center and the Pentagon?

Tests showed that each of the poisoned letters had been spiked with the same Ames strain of bacillus anthracis, first isolated from a cow in Texas in 1981. This ultimately led the F.B.I. to suspect that the culprit might work for or be connected to one of the microbiology laboratories that handled the strain. But as investigators searched for answers, clues faded and doubts deepened. Only a relative handful of epidemiologists and physicians had ever seen a case of anthrax, so how could they be expected to recognize and treat one?

The news media and elected officials at first seemed to be the target. Later, health officials belatedly realized that postal workers were threatened, too. Two Washington, D.C., postal workers died in late October, several weeks after Robert Stevens, a photo editor at The Sun, a tabloid based in Boca Raton, Florida, became the first anthrax fatality. Mail distribution centers in Washington and New Jersey were shut down. Federal officials even briefly debated stopping the delivery of mail across the United States.

It was all profoundly embarrassing for the top scientists and doctors at the federal Centers for Disease Control and Prevention. Initially, they had confidently declared that only people who directly handled unsealed contaminated mail were at risk. But after the postal workers died, doctors realized that even mail sorters and letter carriers could catch the disease. Then, a 61-year-old Bronx woman, who lived alone and worked in a small Manhattan hospital, fell ill and died. Befuddled investigators could not figure out why she might be a target: did she innocently brush against the terrorist? Could a new, more widespread strike be under way? It was only after another woman, a 94-year-old widow in Connecticut, died from anthrax, that health officials concluded that a fatal dose of the disease could be

An agent from the F.B.I.'s Special Investigation Unit, left, and a firefighter from Boca Raton, Florida, conduct anthrax tests on October 11 in Boca Raton at the American Media building. Three people who worked in the building were exposed to the bacteria, and one died.

transmitted by a random letter that had merely crossed paths in a post office with one of the poisoned letters.

As the year came to a close and no new signs of anthrax-poisoned letters appeared, federal health officials privately expressed great relief. Yes, five people were dead; nearly 20 others became sick. But the bioterrorist nightmare that might have killed thousands turned out to be an epidemic that never happened. Calm slowly descended and reports of possible anthrax sightings stopped almost as quickly as they had started.

But this relatively isolated attack was more than enough to expose serious weaknesses in the public health response. A new national effort backed by billions in federal funds was started to better prepare the nation for any future bioterrorist assault. Local health departments, emergency room doctors and others had to be better trained. Millions of doses of anthrax antibiotics and smallpox vaccines were ordered for stockpiling. New laboratories had to be built to handle the deluge of samples that would need early testing in the event of a new scare.

Why the urgency? Federal officials said it was motivated in part by fear of what might have been. "The worst moments for me are realizing that as complicated as this has been and as tragic as it has been for afflicted people, that this is a really small scale event compared to what might happen," said Dr. Julie Gerberding, one of the top officials at the C.D.C. division that supervised the anthrax investigation. "And that's when I have the greatest anxiety and the greatest fear."

—ERIC LIPTON

Traces of anthrax were found in these mailboxes, outside the Princeton post office in West Windsor, New Jersey. October 28, 2001.

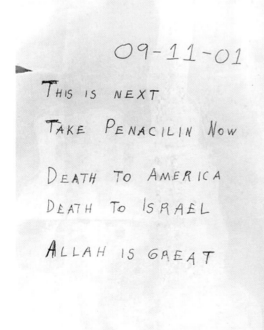

Letter containing anthrax sent to The New York Post.

ANTHRAX AND THE HIJACKERS

The two men identified themselves as pilots when they came to the emergency room of Holy Cross Hospital in Fort Lauderdale, Florida, last June. One had an ugly, dark lesion on his leg that he said he developed after bumping into a suitcase two months earlier. Dr. Christos Tsonas thought the injury was curious, but he cleaned it, prescribed an antibiotic for infection and sent the men away with hardly another thought.

But after September 11, when federal investigators found the medicine among the possessions of one of the hijackers, Ahmed Alhaznawi, Dr. Tsonas reviewed the case and arrived at a new diagnosis. The lesion, he said in an interview this week, "was consistent with cutaneous anthrax."

Dr. Tsonas's comments add to a tantalizing array of circumstantial evidence. Some of the hijackers, including Mr. Alhaznawi, lived and attended flight school near American Media Inc. in Boca Raton, Florida, where the first victim of the anthrax attacks worked. Some of the hijackers also rented apartments from a real estate agent who was the wife of an editor of The Sun, a publication of American Media.

In addition, in October, a pharmacist in Delray Beach, Florida, said he had told the F.B.I. that two of the hijackers, Mohamed Atta and Marwan al-Shehhi, came into the pharmacy looking for something to treat irritations on Mr. Atta's hands.

For his part, Dr. Tsonas said he believed that the hijackers probably did have anthrax.

"What were they doing looking at crop-dusters?" he asked, echoing experts' fears that the hijackers may have wanted to spread lethal germs. "There are too many coincidences."

—WILLIAM J. BROAD AND DAVID JOHNSTON
MARCH 23, 2002

With office buildings on Capitol Hill closed while investigators searched for anthrax contamination on October 19, senators like Patrick J. Leahy, left, and Strom Thurmond, seated, were forced to create meeting spaces out of reception rooms.

ORGANIZING TERROR

*An Egyptian passport photo of
Mohamed Atta. 1996.*

With few exceptions, Mohamed Atta regarded the Americans who crossed his path with the same contempt his father once reserved for his Cairo neighbors. He was polite when he had to be — to rent a car or an airplane — but the mildness recalled by his friends in Egypt and Germany was gone, as was his beard.

He arrived in June at Newark International Airport and would spend the next 15 months in near perpetual motion, earning a pilot's license in Florida during the last six months of 2000, then spending the first nine months of 2001 traveling across the country and at least twice to Europe.

The awful efficiency of the attack demanded a leader with a precise and disciplined temperament, and Mr. Atta apparently filled that role. Federal investigators have told a House committee that in the fall of 2000, as he was in the middle of flight training in Venice, Florida, Mr. Atta received a wire transfer of more than $100,000 from a source in the United Arab Emirates. Investigators believe the source was Mustafa Ahmad, thought to be an alias for Shaykh Said, a finance chief for Osama bin Laden.

For much of 2001, Mr. Atta appeared to make important contacts with other hijackers or conspirators. He traveled twice to Spain, in January and July, and officials are investigating whether he met with Al Qaeda contacts. He also used Florida as a base to move around the United States, including trips to Atlanta, where he rented a plane, to New Jersey, where he may have met with other hijackers, and at least two trips to Las Vegas. Everywhere he went, he made hundreds of cellphone calls and made a point to rent computers for e-mails, including at a Las Vegas computer store, Cyberzone, where customers can play a video game about terrorists with a voice that declares "terrorists win."

While Mr. Atta was considered a perfectionist, he was not infallible. Brad Warrick, owner of a rental agency in South Florida where Mr. Atta returned a car two days before the attack, found an ATM receipt and a white Post-it note that became key evidence. Mr. Atta's decision to wire $4,000 overseas shortly before the attacks left an electronic trail that investigators believe is leading back to Al Qaeda. Finally, authorities found his luggage at Logan Airport in Boston, containing, among other things, his will. It remains unclear if the bag simply missed the connection to his flight.

Or perhaps the introvert, the meticulous planner, the man who believed he was doing God's will, wanted to make certain the world knew his name.

*Mohamed Atta and Abdulaziz Alomari entering and, 20 minutes later,
exiting a Wal-Mart in Scarborough, Maine. September 10, 2001.*

— **BASED ON REPORTING BY NEIL MACFARQUHAR,
JIM YARDLEY AND PAUL ZIELBAUER AND WRITTEN
BY MR. YARDLEY**
OCTOBER 10, 2001

THE NIGHT BEFORE

For their last night on earth, the pair of terrorists stayed at a Comfort Inn on a sterile strip of gas stations and fast-food joints [in South Portland, Maine].

Driving a silver-blue rented Nissan Altima, Mohamed Atta and Abdulaziz Alomari spent at least part of the evening in the most pedestrian of pursuits, mostly along a broad suburban stretch of asphalt called Maine Mall Road: 15 minutes at a Pizza Hut, a quick stop at a gas station and about 20 minutes at a Wal-Mart in Scarborough, the next town.

They also stopped at two automated teller machines. At one, surveillance cameras show Mr. Alomari grinning, while Mr. Atta, who is believed to have been a ringleader of the September 11 terrorist attacks, was stone-faced and sober.

"They did nothing different than almost any other person who visits the state of Maine from out of state," said Stephen McCausland, a spokesman for the Maine Department of Public Safety. "They went to eat, they gassed up their car and they visited Wal-Mart.

"It is eerie to know that these two central figures in this horrific event were here doing those things the night before," Mr. McCausland said.

—**Pam Belluck**
OCTOBER 5, 2001

Twelve hours before flying a plane into the World Trade Center, Abdulaziz Alomari, foreground, and Mohamed Atta, rear at top left, were photographed by a security camera at an A.T.M. in South Portland, Maine. September 10, 2001.

Eight United States athletes carry the American flag during the opening ceremony of the 2002 Winter Olympics. The tattered flag was recovered from the World Trade Center site. Salt Lake City, Utah. February 8, 2002.

"Jihad is the shortest road to Paradise — Harkat-ul-Mujahedeen," says a sign in Urdu in the Malakand district, citing an Islamic militant group. Swat Valley, Pakistan. December 3, 2001.

IV

THE CHALLENGE ABROAD

UNCERTAIN VICTORY

JOHN F. BURNS

To America and the watching world, there were only 16 minutes of doubt — the period between the first and second planes hitting the twin towers. From the instant of the impact with the south tower, it was plain that this was terrorism, not a nightmarish accident. To those with a knowledge of the most virulent strains of Islamic militancy and the way in which they were fueled by a phosphoric hatred for America, it was just as plain that there was, from that moment, a prime suspect, Osama bin Laden. After years of vacillation and avoidance, the United States was finally confronted with the need to go to war.

For nine years before September 11, Osama bin Laden had been moving ever closer to mounting a cataclysmic attack on the United States. Still learning the terrorist's black arts, he began with less ambitious projects. When he finally did strike, America was as stunned as it had been by Pearl Harbor nearly 60 years earlier. But now, as then, America lost little time in responding. Even before President George W. Bush had returned to Washington on the evening of September 11, a war plan was forming. With Al Qaeda operating from sanctuary in Afghanistan, a primary land base in the area was needed, and politics and geography demanded that it be Pakistan, with its 1,400-mile land border abutting the Taliban and Al Qaeda strongholds in southern Afghanistan. On the afternoon of September 11, Pakistan's military intelligence chief, Lt. General Mahmood Ahmed, visiting Washington, was summoned to the State Department and told what quickly became Washington's maxim in marshaling an alliance for its war on terrorism: You are with us, or against us, and woe betide you if you side with the terrorists.

A pro-Taliban supporter listens to speeches given by religious leaders during an anti-American rally. Quetta, Pakistan. October 2, 2001.

VINCENT LAFORET/NYT

Within a week, Pakistan made its choice. Quickly, five airbases across Pakistan were leased to American forces and Pakistan's airspace was opened to American warplanes flying from aircraft carriers in the Arabian Sea and land bases as distant as Diego Garcia 2,500 miles away in the southern reaches of the Indian Ocean. The Pakistani military intelligence agency, I.S.I., began telling the Americans what it knew about the military capabilities of the Taliban and Al Qaeda, and the hideouts favored by their leaders. Pakistani mullahs heading Islamic fundamentalist groups opposing the new alliance of the Pakistani president, General Pervez Musharraf, with America were detained — the first step in what, in the following months, became a concerted drive to break the stranglehold the fundamentalist groups had placed on key areas of Pakistan's public life.

On the night of October 7, the American bombing began. One of the first targets was a compound in Kandahar that served as a home, and headquarters, for the Taliban leader, Mullah Mohammad Omar. His escape that night, after a 10-year-old son and other members of his family were killed, began a long sequence of frustration for American commanders. In the years before September 11, Mullah Omar and Mr. bin Laden had developed a close, even symbiotic relationship, with Mr. bin Laden, improbably, proclaiming Mullah Omar to be the new caliph of the Muslim world, and Mullah Omar, a 43-year-old with little formal education, embracing Mr. bin Laden's notion that Afghanistan could become the base for a Muslim revival that would ultimately destroy American power.

Under the American onslaught, both men disappeared, leaving American commanders chasing elusive sightings for months.

The American war effort was decisive, however, in toppling the Taliban government, killing or scattering thousands of Taliban and Al Qaeda fighters, and ending the dream of Afghanistan becoming the base area for a worldwide Islamic revolution. But even this, for a time, looked like it might be a tougher job than it seemed when the full force of the world's mightiest power was summoned to the task. For several weeks after the bombing began, Taliban defenses, reinforced with Al Qaeda fighters, withstood round-the-clock attacks by B-52's, B-1's, F-18's, F-16's, F-15's and A-10 bombers, among other aircraft types, as well as cruise missiles. But just when it began to look as though the Islamic militants could hold out through the bitter cold of the Afghan winter, on November 13, Taliban front lines north of Kabul collapsed.

By mid-December, nine weeks after the bombing began, the Taliban were routed everywhere, in Kabul, Jalalabad and Kandahar south of the Hindu Kush mountains, in Herat in the west, and in Mazar-i-Sharif and Kunduz in the north. In Kabul, power fell to the Northern Alliance, a coalition of ethnic Tajik, Uzbek and Hazara forces that had, a year earlier, been reduced to pockets of resistance to the Taliban in the north that accounted for barely 10 percent of the country. Across the southern heartland of the Pashtuns, the largest of the country's ethnic groups and the bedrock of support for the Taliban, the reins of authority, such as they were, were seized by local warlords favored by the Americans. The repressive rule of the Taliban, in much of the country, was supplanted by the power of the warlords' guns.

America and its western allies in the war — principally, Britain, France and Germany, along with a phalanx of other

Warplanes from the U.S.S. Theodore Roosevelt in the Arabian Sea. November 30, 2001.

POOL PHOTO BY ED WRAY

NATO nations — moved rapidly to fill the power vacuum left by the Taliban. After a conference in Bonn, Afghan delegates drawn from across the spectrum of anti-Taliban groups agreed, after lengthy wrangling, to the formation of an interim government under the leadership of a Pashtun tribal leader favored by the United States, Hamid Karzai. But with Pashtuns still deeply divided among themselves after the fall of the Taliban, the real power in the new government belonged to Tajik leaders from the Northern Alliance, who took the key portfolios of interior, defense and foreign affairs.

From its inauguration in late December, the Karzai government's role was to begin a 30-month transition to elections in June 2004. Its own lifespan was limited to the first six months, during which a traditional Afghan consultative body, a loya jirga, was to agree on a broader-based provisional government. The Karzai ministry got an early lift when a conference of the world's wealthiest nations, meeting in Tokyo in January, pledged an initial $4.5 billion to a fund for the country's reconstruction. The hope was these funds would give the new government, lacking just about everything else that lends authority to a nation's rulers, including an army loyal to the state, the influence needed to keep the warlords at bay.

But from early on, the signs were that the new government's writ ran only about as far as the city limits of Kabul. The real underpinning for its authority came from a 4,500-member British-led international military brigade, known as the International Security Assistance Force. But its jurisdiction was limited to the Kabul district, and the western powers were reluctant to agree to what Mr. Karzai told them, repeatedly, was the minimal condition for Afghanistan's successful transition to stability: An expanded international force of 20,000 to 30,000 troops, capable of restraining the warlords and creating conditions, beyond Kabul, where the ambitious reconstruction plans could be turned into reality.

Even in Kabul, there were signs of serious rifts within the government. Barely two months after the new government took office, one of its ministers, Abdul Rahman, was assassinated at Kabul airport in what Mr. Karzai called a conspiracy among other senior government officials. The official version was that the murder resulted from personal grievances against Mr. Rahman, a Tajik who had quit the Northern Alliance during the period of Taliban rule to join the Pashtuns pressing for the restoration of the former king, Mohammed Zahir Shah, a Pashtun who has lived for nearly 30 years in Rome. But the future role of the monarchy, favored by many Pashtuns but bitterly opposed by some powerful Tajiks, was one of many fault lines running through the country in the wake of the Taliban.

Women wait for food to be distributed at a refugee camp in northern Afghanistan. October 1, 2001.

JAMES HILL FOR NYT

As the Karzai government stumbled onwards, there were signs that the Taliban and Al Qaeda, though ousted from the cities, were still capable of mustering a sizable force in the hinterland. In March, a 1,200-person American infantry force was committed to battle in the first major ground action of the war, against a concentration of Taliban and Al Qaeda fighters in the Shah-i-Kot valley 90 miles south of Kabul. Eight Americans were killed, along with three fighters from allied Afghan forces, and American commanders warned that there were other pockets of resistance elsewhere in the country that could require an American military presence for months to come.

Nor was the news from Pakistan everything the United States wanted to hear. Early in the year, General Musharraf, shunned as a military usurper before September 11, was greeted as a stalwart friend of the United States at the White House, where President Bush applauded him for his courage. But at home, the Islamic militants were just then setting out to prove that their brutality was far from over. On February 21, a videotape delivered to the F.B.I. in Karachi showed a militant group in the city beheading Daniel Pearl, a Wall Street Journal reporter who had been kidnapped in the city four weeks earlier. On March 17, two militants tossed grenades into a Sunday morning service at a Protestant church in Islamabad, the Pakistani capital, killing five people, including the wife and 17-year-old daughter of an American diplomat, and injuring more than 40 others.

Six months after September 11, the hard truth was that the United States and its allies had demolished the Taliban as a government, without eradicating them entirely as a force in the country's life. At the same time, they had denied to Al Qaeda the secure base of operations it had established in Afghanistan, while barely beginning the task of uprooting an Al Qaeda network that American counterterrorism experts have calculated extends to as many as 60 other countries. In Pakistan, although the government had vowed to crush Islamic militancy after years of encouraging it, the militants had shown that they had fangs that were not going to be so easily pulled. To paraphrase Winston Churchill at a critical juncture in another war, the spring of 2002 seemed to mark not the end of the American war on terrorism, nor even the beginning of the end, but perhaps only the end of the beginning.

—*From Kabul*

A Marine CH-53E Super Stallion helicopter flies over Camp Rhino in southern Afghanistan. December 8, 2001.

THE HOLY WAR AGAINST AMERICA

Gangs of furious protesters roamed the streets of Quetta today, smashing and burning anything that appeared American or Western on a day when anger over the airstrikes on Afghanistan swept Pakistan, the world's second-most-populous Islamic nation.

The gangs in Quetta, estimated at 10,000 to 15,000 strong by the police, were the most violent. They threw rocks at the headquarters of the United Nations refugee agency near the airport and then set fire to the Unicef office nearby, destroying five cars.

—DOUGLAS FRANTZ
OCTOBER 9, 2001

Taliban supporters at a rally denouncing the United States. Islamabad, Pakistan. September 28, 2001.

THE CHALLENGE ABROAD

A boy with a toy pistol is held aloft by an anti-American crowd at a rally. Rawalpindi, Pakistan. October 5, 2001.

ROBERT NICKELSBERG/GETTY IMAGES

RUTH FREMSON/NYT

A demonstrator catches fire as an American flag goes up in flames. The police fired tear gas to control the crowds, which numbered up to 1,000. Peshawar, Pakistan. October 8, 2001.

The mother of Hamid Ullah, 13, grieves over his body in an ambulance following an anti-American protest. Kushlaq, Pakistan. October 9, 2001.

ISLAM ABLAZE

During the first week of American airstrikes, Quetta was a stick of dynamite with the fuse burning. Thousands of protesters rampaged through the streets, shouting anti-American slogans, smashing windows and torching shops and cinemas. Five people were killed by the police here and in a nearby village, and businesses were closed for days.

— **DOUGLAS FRANTZ**
OCTOBER 9, 2001

Osama bin Laden in Afghanistan, April 1998.

OSAMA BIN LADEN

His face is everywhere and nowhere. He was born fabulously rich but is thought to live in desert caves. He seems a soft-spoken ascetic yet he could be the instigator of mass murder. He is an outcast from family, country and religion yet is beloved by millions for his holy war against America.

The myths and realities of Osama bin Laden swirl together like the smoke over the ruins of the World Trade Center and its thousands of dead. Who is this man?

To the United States government, the 44-year-old Saudi exile is the most wanted fugitive in history, the founder and leader of a terrorist network known as Al Qaeda (The Base), which has in a decade trained [many thousands of] militants in Sudan and Afghanistan and posted them to perhaps 50 countries to await their turn to strike. And strike they have, American officials assert, with bin Laden plans, money or inspiration behind the bombings of the trade center in 1993 (6 dead), two American embassies in Africa in 1998 (224 dead) and the destroyer Cole in Yemen in 2000 (17 dead), and the jetliners that collapsed the trade center towers, damaged the Pentagon and crashed in Pennsylvania on September 11 [several thousands feared dead].

To millions of Americans, who have seen his face on television daily and on the magazine covers and front pages of newspapers, Mr. bin Laden is the mask of evil; in many minds he is already guilty of killing thousands, although he has not been found, let alone tried.

To millions in the Islamic world who hate America for what they regard as its decadent culture and imperial government, he is a hero who shunned the easy life to battle the infidels for Allah, who has justified killings with arcane interpretations of the Koran, and carried them out.

To the Taliban, the extremist Islamic clerics who have ruled Afghanistan and given him haven since 1996, he is a spiritual and political ally and a source of money, but one whose presence has become a growing liability.

And to those closest to him, there is yet another man — the family man who takes his 3 wives and 15 children from cave to cave, moving every night or two, with dozens of bodyguards — one a bin Laden double — in a desert-roving caravan of land cruisers armed with missiles.

Mr. bin Laden went from a childhood of lofty privilege and education in Saudi Arabia to being galvanized by the war against the Soviets in Afghanistan in the 1980's. Investigators say he went to Sudan for five years in the early 1990's to build his network and multiply his fortune, then to Afghanistan, to wage war.

Along the way, the young man — one of 52 children of an immigrant Yemeni bricklayer who became Saudi Arabia's richest building contractor — moved from boyish piety to youthful carousing in the bars of Beirut, then back to Islamic fervor.

Osama bin Laden (rhymes with sadden) was born in 1957 in Saudi Arabia, the 17th of 24 sons in a family of immigrants. His mother was Syrian or Palestinian, one of many wives of Mohammed bin Oud bin Laden, who came from neighboring Yemen in 1932 and, through friendship with the country's founder, King Abdel Aziz al-Saud, won contracts to build the infrastructure of roads and refurbish the shrines at Mecca and Medina, Islam's holiest places. The Saudi Binladen Group today has 35,000 employees worldwide and $5 billion in assets.

Osama was 11 or 12 when his father died in a plane crash near San Antonio in 1968. It is unclear how much he inherited — reports vary from $20 million or $80 million to as high as $300 million — but he was wealthy beyond dreams as a boy. He grew tall and lean — eventually reaching 6 feet 5 inches — and towered over classmates and friends.

"He's not very sophisticated politically or organizationally," said a former bin Laden associate whose nom de guerre was Abdullah Anas. "But he's an activist with great imagination. He ate very little. He slept very little. He'd give you his clothes. He'd give you his money."

American agents first came upon the global ambitions of Mr. bin Laden in 1993 while investigating the World Trade Center bombing, though evidence of his direct involvement is not conclusive.

In 1994, Saudi Arabia revoked his citizenship and his family disowned him. Islamic leaders in other countries, offended that he used Islam to justify murder, disavowed him.

By then, American officials regarded Mr. bin Laden as a stateless sponsor of terrorism. Washington pressed Sudan to expel him, and in 1996 succeeded. He went back to Afghanistan. Before long, the Taliban was letting him use the country as what Mr. Anas called a "jihad camp for the world."

—**ROBERT D. MCFADDEN**
SEPTEMBER 30, 2001

CREED OF THE WAHHABIS

The faith that drives Osama bin Laden and his followers is a particularly austere and conservative brand of Islam known as Wahhabism, which was instrumental in creating the Saudi monarchy, and if sufficiently alienated, could tear it down.

Throughout the sect's history, the Wahhabis have fiercely opposed anything they viewed as bida, an Arabic word, usually muttered as a curse, for any change or modernization that deviates from the fundamental teachings of the Koran.

The telephone, radio broadcasts and public education for women were at one point condemned as innovations wrought by the Devil. Riots ensued over the introduction of television in 1965, and were quelled only after the police fired on demonstrators. Similar tensions exist today. A recent ruling suggested that the music played as mobile phone rings should be outlawed on religious grounds.

Whenever the forces of change prevailed, it was usually with the argument that the novelty could help propagate the Koran. When that argument fell flat, change stalled. So, for example, there are no movie theaters in Saudi Arabia — they would promote the unhealthy mingling of the sexes — and women are banned from driving.

But above all, the Wahhabis believe their faith should spread, not giving ground in any place they have conquered. Thus Saudi Arabia was a main financial backer of the mujahedeen fighting to expel the godless Communists from Muslim Afghanistan, and Mr. bin Laden became the public's poster boy for that cause.

The ferocity with which the Wahhabis fight for their cause is legend. One Arab historian described followers of the sect, founded in the 18th century, as they engaged in battle: "I have seen them hurl themselves on their enemies, utterly fearless of death, not caring how many fall, advancing rank after rank with only one desire — the defeat and annihilation of the enemy. They normally give no quarter, sparing neither boys nor old men."

— NEIL MACFARQUHAR
OCTOBER 7, 2001

A translated example of leaflets dropped in Afghanistan offering a bounty for Mr. bin Laden and a senior aide, Ayman al-Zawahiri.

Frame grabs from a videotape of Mr. bin Laden talking about the terrorist attacks. United States officials translated audio conversation from Arabic to English. Location undisclosed. Released December 13, 2001.

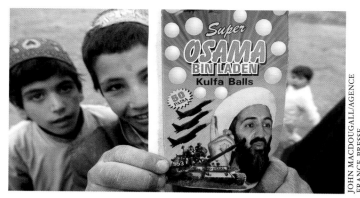

JOHN MACDOUGALL/AGENCE FRANCE-PRESSE

Young Afghan boys show off a package of sweets named for Osama bin Laden. Kandahar, Afghanistan. December 14, 2001.

SELLING THEIR HERO

Glossy posters of Osama bin Laden atop a white stallion or brandishing a Kalashnikov are selling as fast as they are printed in Quetta's chaotic bazaar. Osama T-shirts and chocolates wrapped in his bearded face are popular, too.

Support for Mr. bin Laden and sympathy for ordinary Afghans being subjected to withering American bombing remain high in Pakistan, particularly here in the border region, which is dominated by tribal loyalties and religious firebrands.

Many people who knew little or nothing of the most wanted man in the world before September 11 now regard him as a hero, not because of the attacks on the United States, but because the huge campaign to capture or kill him has elevated his stature.

—DOUGLAS FRANTZ
OCTOBER 22, 2001

ARIF ALI/AGENCE FRANCE-PRESSE

A man samples a fragrance named for the Qaeda leader. Lahore, Pakistan. December 21, 2001.

DADANG TRI/REUTERS

Street traders in Jakarta, Indonesia. November 25, 2001.

Taliban soldiers keep a sharp watch on foreign journalists during a tour of Kandahar. Crowds mobbed the journalists, and some people shouted anti-American slogans. Kandahar, Afghanistan. November 3, 2001.

Taliban soldiers on the day after American and British airstrikes began. Kabul, Afghanistan. October 8, 2001.

THE TALIBAN

"Sometimes, I thought the Taliban were from another century," [Peter] Goossens [the World Food Program's deputy director in Afghanistan] said. "And sometimes I thought they were from another planet."

The Taliban stood as the embodiment of a nation, but succeeded only in gaining the allegiance of their own ethnic group, the Pashtuns, and in the end they lost that, too. It is now clear that as the end drew closer, only a combination of drugs, Pakistani help and the largesse of the world's most wanted man kept them afloat.

—**DEXTER FILKINS**
DECEMBER 31, 2001

JAMES HILL FOR NYT

For now, the front lines remain largely where they were a month ago, with about 15,000 forces of the Northern Alliance, the main opposition group, arrayed against Taliban forces estimated at 40,000 throughout the country.

Operating without the benefit of an active resistance in the south, the Pentagon has sought to make the best of what friendly forces it can use on the ground: the Northern Alliance, a loose coalition of ethnic Uzbeks and Tajiks who have been fighting the Taliban in the northern part of the country.

—**Michael R. Gordon**
NOVEMBER 8, 2001

Uniformed Northern Alliance reservists march on a parched plain outside of Khwaja Bahaouddin in northern Afghanistan. October 5, 2001.

PHOTOGRAPHS BY STEPHEN CROWLEY/NYT

A sailor approaches the U.S.S. Theodore Roosevelt. Norfolk, Virginia. September 19, 2001.

GOING TO WAR

Quietly, in the month of war, the United States has nearly doubled the number of American military forces involved, underscoring the deepening commitment to a conflict that is already costing tens of millions of dollars a day, with those costs rising daily.

Today, more than 50,000 American soldiers, sailors, airmen and marines are deployed across a region stretching from the Red Sea to the Indian Ocean, Pentagon officials said. Thousands more are expected to join the effort along with still more warplanes and other material in still more countries surrounding Afghanistan.

Roughly half of the total American forces — about 25,000 — are aboard naval vessels operating in the northern Arabian Sea, but significantly higher numbers than the Pentagon has previously disclosed are flowing into bases around the region, including several hundred soldiers and marines in Pakistan.

More than 400 American aircraft — including sea- and land-based fighter jets and long-range bombers — are already flying scores of combat missions a day, supported by reconnaissance aircraft, cargo jets and aerial refuelers in elaborately choreographed operations. That includes aircraft continuing to patrol the "no flight" zones over southern and northern Iraq, some of which have been diverted to the war.

In addition, nearly two dozen American ships are operating in the North Arabian Sea, including nuclear-powered submarines, an amphibious assault group carrying the 15th Marine Expeditionary Unit and two aircraft carriers, the Theodore Roosevelt and the Carl Vinson. A third carrier, the Kitty Hawk, is also in the area, carrying an undisclosed number of Special Operations helicopters and soldiers.

The American forces are spread out in a way that reflects diplomatic sensitivities in several countries about accepting large numbers of American troops and aircraft.

— **MICHAEL R. GORDON**
NOVEMBER 8, 2001

A crew member gets out of the way as a fighter jet takes off from the deck of the U.S.S. Theodore Roosevelt. Off Norfolk, Virginia. September 19, 2001.

Crossing by air over the hills into Afghanistan from Tajikistan, American Special Operations soldiers keep watch from the open back end of an Army Special Forces Chinook helicopter, near Khwaja Bahuaddin, Afghanistan. November 15, 2001.

SCORCHED EARTH

Although the American military is famous for its high-technology precision weapons, the Pentagon has relied on some of its oldest arms to attack Taliban ground forces and try to shatter their will to fight.

B-52 bombers, upgraded since the Vietnam War, are dropping dozens of 500-pound unguided bombs on Taliban troops dug in along the front lines. Lumbering AC-130 Spectre gunships rain heavy caliber machine-gun and cannon fire down on enemy positions as they did in Southeast Asia more than three decades ago.

There are certain places on the battlefield where commanders want the maximum punishment, not precision. Last weekend, for instance, the Air Force hit front-line Taliban forces with two of the 15,000-pound BLU-82 daisy cutter bombs — one of the most powerful conventional weapons in the American arsenal that also dates from Vietnam. The bombs can obliterate an area hundreds of yards in diameter.

—MICHAEL R. GORDON
NOVEMBER 8, 2001

American Special Forces soldiers in position at the Qala Jangi fortress before fighting Taliban prisoners inside. Near Mazar-i-Sharif, Afghanistan. November 26, 2001.

"We have had much success today against the Taliban," said Mamoor Hassan, a senior alliance commander, as the fighting wound down toward sunset. "We have taken the Taliban's front lines, and we have killed a lot of Taliban soldiers. Tomorrow we will try again."

—DEXTER FILKINS
NOVEMBER 11, 2001

Northern Alliance troops walk over the site of a battle with Taliban prisoners at the Qala Jangi fortress. Near Mazar-i-Sharif, Afghanistan. November 28, 2001.

Northern Alliance troops drag a wounded Taliban soldier out of a ditch on the front lines on the way to Kabul. After he begs for his life, they pull him to his feet, shoot him in the chest and beat him with a rifle butt and a rocket-propelled-grenade launcher. November 12, 2001.

PHOTOGRAPHS BY TYLER HICKS/GETTY IMAGES, FOR NYT

THE EXECUTION

Near an abandoned Taliban bunker, Northern Alliance soldiers dragged a wounded Taliban soldier out of a ditch today. As the terrified man begged for his life, the alliance soldiers pulled him to his feet.

They searched him and emptied his pockets. Then, one soldier fired two bursts from his rifle into the man's chest. A second soldier beat the lifeless body with his rifle butt. A third repeatedly smashed a rocket-propelled-grenade launcher into the man's head.

The killing occurred minutes after Northern Alliance soldiers, advancing toward Kabul, surged deep into Taliban territory. They chose to celebrate with executions.

The killings here suggested that alliance soldiers might prove difficult to control as their victories build.

Alliance soldiers reacted to the corpses in different ways. Nearly all stopped and gazed at the dead. Some searched for valuables. One, in a more dignified gesture, placed a cloth over a corpse.

— **DAVID ROHDE**
NOVEMBER 13, 2001

In a coordinated effort, American jets pounded Taliban positions. By midafternoon, mushroom clouds from bombs and shells lined the horizon, and the contrails of the American planes marked the skies in long, white streaks.

—**Dexter Filkins**
NOVEMBER 11, 2001

A man stops to pray by the road during an attack of two American jets circling Taliban positions. Near Desti Qala, Afghanistan. November 11, 2001.

AN AWESOME LAND

The natural world looms large in Afghanistan and its landscape seems bound up in all its parts. The faces of its people, now captured in a thousand photographs, seem merely the human reflections of the country's geography: all crags and fissures, desiccated and rough.

To picture the war being fought here, imagine fighting in the Grand Canyon or Escalante National Monument, or perhaps even on the moon, in the boulders and crevasses, amid stones so large and laid at such odd angles that they appear to have been placed by some divine hand.

—**DEXTER FILKINS**
NOVEMBER 9, 2001

CHANG W. LEE/NYT

The road in Tangi Tashqurghan, clogged by rubble from American bombing, was made passable by three enterprising Afghans. December 15, 2001.

Eastern Shura fighters watch as U.S. B-52's bomb an area of the Tora Bora mountains. December 9, 2001.

STEPHEN CROWLEY/NYT

"We are resupplying the opposition with ammunition, with food, with blankets," General Richard B. Myers, [the chairman of the Joint Chiefs of Staff] said, "[and,] we hope in the not-too-distant future, with cold weather gear. The fighting forces on the side of the opposition on our side will be much better prepared for winter than will the Taliban."

—**MICHAEL R. GORDON**
NOVEMBER 8, 2001

A Northern Alliance sentry with a rocket-propelled-grenade launcher. Salong, Afghanistan. November 9, 2001.

Abdul Haq, a commander in Afghanistan's war against the Soviets, during an interview in his home. Peshawar, Pakistan. October 1, 2001.

RUTH FREMSON/NYT

DISUNITED ALLIES

The Mayday from Afghanistan arrived at Central Intelligence Agency headquarters on October 18.

Robert C. McFarlane, Ronald Reagan's national security adviser, was on the line and he had bad news. Abdul Haq was in Afghanistan and surrounded by Taliban troops. He needed help and fast.

The C.I.A. and a liaison officer from the United States Central Command took down Mr. Haq's coordinates.

An airstrike was ordered, Mr. McFarlane said. But it was too late. Hours later, the Taliban announced that it had captured and executed Mr. Haq.

Patriotism, vengeance and dreams of glory had driven Mr. Haq out of exile and back into Afghanistan. His country, his wife and his son had died at the hands of his enemies. He wanted to fight back. He was a middle-aged man on a mule, a privately financed freelancer trying to overthrow the Taliban.

The State Department lauded him. "Throughout his life, this gentleman has been a voice for the establishment of broad-based government for his country," the State Department spokesman, Richard Boucher, said.

—**MICHAEL R. GORDON AND TIM WEINER**
OCTOBER 27, 2001

A Northern Alliance soldier runs for cover during an American bomb attack. Deu Saraka, Afghanistan. October 22, 2001.

The Northern Alliance remains a largely untested force, and the difficulties of marshaling it, or any faction, were clear enough at the Pentagon today. "There is not one 'the' Northern Alliance," the Pentagon spokeswoman, Victoria Clarke, said. "There are different factions. And there are tribes in the south. And there are people within the Taliban itself that oppose the Taliban regime."

—**MICHAEL R. GORDON**
NOVEMBER 8, 2001

American Marines at their basecamp on the grounds of Kandahar International Airport. December 16, 2001.

SEIZING KANDAHAR AIRPORT

A vanguard of marines in armored vehicles rolled into the airport outside of Kandahar early today, consolidating control over a scene of intense fighting against the Taliban and clearing the way for deliveries of supplies and aid.

Officers said the airport, once repaired, would provide a better, more centrally located base of operations than the isolated, rudimentary airstrip they have been using.

Marine officers said the immediate aim was to root out any isolated pockets of Taliban and Al Qaeda fighters, some of whom continue to resist despite the takeover of Kandahar by Pashtun factions led by Hamid Karzai, the designated leader of Afghanistan's new government.

—STEVEN LEE MYERS
DECEMBER 14, 2001

Marines at the Kandahar airport on December 26, 2001.

SENSORS AND TARGETS

American forces seeking the hide-outs of Osama bin Laden are being equipped with sophisticated new technology — an array of sensors — that can pierce darkness, bad weather and as much as 100 feet of solid rock, homing in on heat, magnetic fields, vibrations and other faint cues.

The devices, borne by aircraft, towed behind vehicles or carried by soldiers, can sense slight traces of heat on a cold mountainside, the hum of a buried generator, the magnetic signals from electrical wires.

The sophisticated surveillance equipment could be particularly valuable, government officials say, now that the fast-moving military campaign in Afghanistan has forced leaders of Al Qaeda and the Taliban to shun radios and mobile phones, which had been routinely intercepted by electronic sensors on American spy planes.

As it happens, the heat-sensing devices will work with increasing efficiency as cold weather tightens its grip in the region. Scientists who helped develop the equipment say the slightest hint of warm air escaping from a tunnel or cave will stand out like a beacon from miles away.

"The popular conception seems to be that bin Laden and his 40 thieves are in the bottom of some deep cavern, and if we can just find the secret cavern, then the war will be over," said John E. Pike, director of GlobalSecurity.org, a private group whose Web site reports on advances in military technology. "But these guys are undoubtedly scattered all over the place — some in town, some up in the hills, some in houses, others in tunnels."

— **ANDREW C. REVKIN**
NOVEMBER 22, 2001

Refining the Air Campaign

Advances in technology since the 1999 Kosovo campaign have allowed airstrikes to hit more targets with greater accuracy and have reduced risks to pilots.

BOMBERS

Fly at altitudes of up to 35,000 feet, out of the range of antiaircraft fire. Several different bombers and fighters are now equipped with satellite- and laser-guided bombs that use target data from drones and ground spotters.
Shown: B-52 Stratofortress.

UNMANNED SURVEILLANCE DRONES

Transmit high-definition video, still images and radar data via satellite to ground control stations out of the area of battle. Shown: RQ-1 Predator.

⊕ LASER TARGET DESIGNATION

LOCATING THE TARGET The binoculars measure the time it takes pulses of light to travel to the target and back, giving precise range data for the target.

GUIDING BOMBS The pulse repetition frequency of the target laser is matched to the detector in the laser-guided bomb to be used, and the bomb follows the laser into the target.

SPOTTERS ON THE GROUND

Special Operations forces use laser rangefinder binoculars to pinpoint targets and then transmit coordinates to the bombers and fighters by phone or computer.

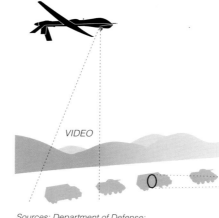

VIDEO

LASER

Sources: Department of Defense; Federation of American Scientists

Below the Surface

There are innumerable caves and tunnels in Afghanistan, but Osama bin Laden was said to be moving from cave to cave along the Pakistan border.

Tora Bora

Mr. bin Laden moved to this base for Afghan rebels after being forced to leave Sudan.

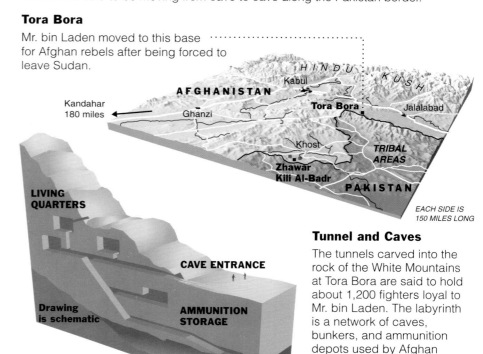

Kandahar 180 miles

EACH SIDE IS 150 MILES LONG

LIVING QUARTERS

CAVE ENTRANCE

Drawing is schematic

AMMUNITION STORAGE

Tunnel and Caves

The tunnels carved into the rock of the White Mountains at Tora Bora are said to hold about 1,200 fighters loyal to Mr. bin Laden. The labyrinth is a network of caves, bunkers, and ammunition depots used by Afghan rebels who fought the Soviet Union in the 1980's. Their construction was partly financed by aid from the United States.

Sources: Defense Department; "Underground Combat: Stereophonic Blasting, Tunnel Rats, and the Soviet-Afghan War" by Retired Lt. Col. Lester W. Grau and Ali Ahmad

ANATOMY OF A MOUNTAIN BUNKER

Some of the man-made burrows deep inside mountains in Afghanistan were upgraded by Al Qaeda in recent years. Roomier and with more amenities than naturally formed caves, bunkers like this may be housing Osama bin Laden and his soldiers.

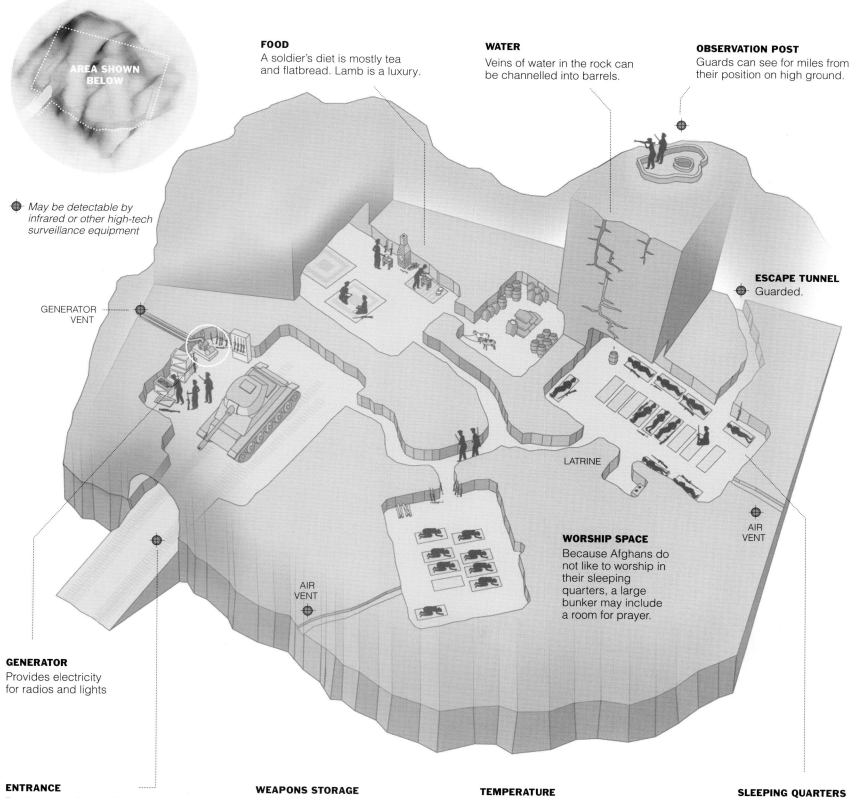

AREA SHOWN BELOW

FOOD
A soldier's diet is mostly tea and flatbread. Lamb is a luxury.

WATER
Veins of water in the rock can be channelled into barrels.

OBSERVATION POST
Guards can see for miles from their position on high ground.

May be detectable by infrared or other high-tech surveillance equipment

GENERATOR VENT

ESCAPE TUNNEL
Guarded.

LATRINE

AIR VENT

AIR VENT

WORSHIP SPACE
Because Afghans do not like to worship in their sleeping quarters, a large bunker may include a room for prayer.

GENERATOR
Provides electricity for radios and lights

ENTRANCE
Bunkers are often built with a rocky overhang above openings, so they cannot be glimpsed in satellite pictures. All entrances and exits are guarded.

WEAPONS STORAGE
Weapons may include tanks, rocket-propelled grenades, multiple rocket-launchers, antiaircraft machine guns, rifles and smaller arms.

TEMPERATURE
Because a bunker is deep inside a mountain, it is protected from extreme weather. Even in winter, bunkers at low altitudes generally remain at 40 to 50 degrees.

SLEEPING QUARTERS
Soldiers sleep on the rock floor. A pit dug in the ground serves as a latrine.

Sources: Jack Shroder and Thomas E. Gouttierre, University of Nebraska at Omaha; Defense Department; U.S. Army Foreign Military Studies Office

HANNAH FAIRFIELD; ILLUSTRATION BY JOHN PAPASIAN/NYT

The bodies of Taliban prisoners lie strewn across the inside of the fort at Qala Jangi near Mazar-i-Sharif. November 28, 2001.

JAMES HILL FOR NYT

THE FATE OF THE TALIBAN

And so the Taliban, the radical Islamic movement, died here at the outskirts of Kandahar, seven years after it came to life in nearly the same spot. It had risen from the desert, forcing itself through a historical opening left by the breakup of the Soviet Union, the opportunism of Afghanistan's neighbors, and the growing appeal of radical Islam in a world shorn of its cold war faiths.

Full of itself, the Taliban flourished outside the gaze of the world's remaining superpower, the United States, finally giving succor to the terrorists that would invite its own doom. As a revolutionary movement, the Taliban burned hot and fast.

—**DEXTER FILKINS**
DECEMBER 31, 2001

Northern Alliance troops near Amirabad watch as a convoy of surrendering Taliban soldiers from Kunduz passes through the front lines. November 24, 2001.

Up to 4,000 Taliban fighters who surrendered at Kunduz, including some Pakistanis and possibly other foreign volunteers, were taken by truck and crowded into a prison hundreds of miles to the west. One of the prisoners said at least 13 people had suffocated during the trip in tightly packed container trucks. Shibarghan, Afghanistan. December 1, 2001.

Taliban prisoners, many of them foreigners from the Arab world, Pakistan and the Central Asian republics of the former Soviet Union, in the prison controlled by the Northern Alliance. Shibarghan, Afghanistan. December 6, 2001.

VANQUISHED FIGHTERS

In the month since the collapse of the Taliban government in Afghanistan, nearly 3,500 former Taliban fighters have been held in a prison built for 800, under conditions that are raising alarm among international aid groups.

The International Committee of the Red Cross, which has visited and registered prisoners here in Shibarghan, first raised concern about overcrowding and unsanitary conditions last week, after a prisoner fell sick and died in one of the cells. Dozens more, the agency said, have fallen ill with dysentery.

The concerns about prisoners held by [General Abdul Rashid Dostum, Afghanistan's deputy defense minister, who has a reputation for brutality] follow unconfirmed reports that anti-Taliban troops killed some of them last month as they were being transported from the town of Kunduz to the prison of Shibarghan, General Dostum's hometown. The shipping containers holding the prisoners stopped overnight at Qala Zeina, the fortified western gates to the city of Mazar-i-Sharif and, according to some survivors, troops opened fire.

—**CARLOTTA GALL WITH MARK LANDLER**
JANUARY 5, 2002

Counting Prisoners

The actual number of prisoners now held by anti-Taliban forces remains something of a mystery. The International Committee for the Red Cross says it has visited about 700 prisoners at 15 various sites but concedes that this number is a fraction of the real total.

"The number of prisoners is impossible to estimate," said Michael Kleiner, a spokesman for the committee's office in Kabul. "Without a government in place it is impossible to know where people are being detained."

—Steven Lee Myers with James Dao
December 15, 2001

A warehouse in the town of Khawai in Nangarhar province where 155 Taliban fighters are imprisoned. On the left, a man reads from the Koran. November 21, 2001.

THE CHALLENGE ABROAD

183

John Walker Lindh after his capture in the basement of the Qala Jangi fortress on December 1, 2001.

UNLIKELY FOES

Shortly before he left for Afghanistan, Johnny Micheal Spann sent an e-mail message to his parents back in Winfield, Alabama.

"What everyone needs to understand is these fellows hate you," wrote Mr. Spann, a Central Intelligence Agency officer. "They hate you because you are an American. Support your government and your military, especially when the bodies start coming home."

Mr. Spann, 32, the first American killed by the enemy, was buried today at Arlington National Cemetery, where he had loved to walk among the headstones of the country's fallen heroes. What he was doing in the moments before he died was clear, although accounts of how he died vary. He was interrogating Taliban prisoners, and one was John Walker Lindh. Minutes after he asked questions that elicited only silence, Mr. Spann was killed in a chaotic prison uprising. Mr. Lindh was wounded, hid in a prison basement and was captured seven days later. Now a "battlefield detainee" in a desert Marine base in southern Afghanistan, Mr. Lindh has begun to provide useful information to American officials.

It is their encounter — a videotaped face-off between countrymen and enemies, between a secret soldier from the small-town South and a self-proclaimed seeker of "a true Islamic state" from a wealthy San Francisco suburb — that has Americans fixating on a particularly painful moment in the war. It was an unthinkable confrontation between two young Americans, one fighting for his country, the other, by all appearances, against it.

— BLAINE HARDEN WITH KEVIN SACK
DECEMBER 11, 2001

Johnny Micheal Spann, killed during the prison uprising in Mazar-i-Sharif, Afghanistan.

A caisson carrying the casket of the C.I.A.'s Johnny Micheal Spann makes its way to the grave site. Spann was the first American killed in combat action in Afghanistan. Arlington National Cemetery, Virginia. December 10, 2001.

Taliban detainees and military police officers in a holding area during in-processing. Photographs such as this one prompted harsh criticism, and led the International Committee of the Red Cross and Amnesty International to ask that the U.S. classify the detainees as prisoners of war and abide by the rules of the Geneva Convention. Camp X-Ray at Naval Base Guantánamo Bay, Cuba. January 11, 2002.

A NATION CHALLENGED

GUANTÁNAMO BAY

A C-17 Globemaster cargo plane carrying 20 heavily guarded Taliban and Al Qaeda prisoners left a Marine Corps base in southern Afghanistan today on its way to the United States naval base at Guantánamo Bay, Cuba, the first wave of hundreds of detainees who will be held there.

The Pentagon provided few details about the flight, but senior military officials said more than 40 specially trained military police officers guarded the prisoners on the flight, which was expected to make one stop before reaching Cuba, possibly as early as [the morning of January 11].

The prisoners, their hands and feet shackled and their heads covered by hoods, were loaded single file onto the plane at Kandahar Airport. Pentagon officials said some prisoners might also be sedated during the more-than-20-hour flight, but it was not clear whether that had happened.

A Pentagon official said that the United States did not consider the detainees prisoners of war, but that they were still being afforded the protections under the Geneva Convention guidelines.

At Guantánamo Bay, the prisoners will be taken to a makeshift detention center known as Camp X-Ray, where they will be locked in 6-by-8-foot cages made of concrete and chain-link fence to await intensive interrogation and, possibly, trial before military tribunals.

Amnesty International issued a statement today saying that sedating prisoners or shackling them for an entire flight would violate international standards prohibiting "cruel, inhuman or degrading" treatment.

[Secretary of Defense Donald H.] Rumsfeld said today that he did not know how the prisoners would be restrained during the flight. But he defended the use of strong measures, saying the Pentagon had closely studied violent uprisings by Taliban and Al Qaeda prisoners held in the northern Afghan city of Mazar-i-Sharif and in Pakistan.

—JAMES DAO
JANUARY 11, 2002

OPERATION ANACONDA

Trapped by intense hostile fire and unable to evacuate their wounded for 12 hours, American Special Operations forces fought off an Al Qaeda ambush in some of the most grueling and gruesome combat of the five-month-old war in Afghanistan, officials said today.

When it was over on Monday, the bodies of seven American servicemen and 11 wounded comrades were lifted off the battlefield under guard of American combat aircraft. The machine guns and cannon of AC-130's drove back the advancing fighters — but not before commanders monitoring airborne surveillance video had seen Al Qaeda fighters dragging off an American serviceman to his death, military officials said.

Some of the heaviest fighting of the five-month war also brought the heaviest American combat losses, with Pentagon officials and senior military officers describing a battlefield where the topography itself was as hostile as the adversary — allowing opposing fighters, who seemed willing to fight to the death rather than surrender, to charge and then retreat to fortified caves and trenches.

— THOM SHANKER
MARCH 6, 2002

The largest American-led ground operation of the five-month war is being waged across a 60-square-mile swath of snowcapped mountains and deep valleys, roughly twice the size of Manhattan.

Unlike earlier battles in this war, there is no single front line in the Shah-i-Kot Valley; there is no single concentration of adversaries under siege. Instead, enemy fighters were scattered in handfuls and by the score in caves and trenches and some village structures all across the combat zone.

One military planner compared the area of combat to a pepperoni pizza in a box: the pepperonis were groups of enemy fighters. The box was the American-led coalition blocking force. The American plan was to move allied and American fighters by land and by air toward the enemy clusters for direct engagement and to drive them outward toward the blocking force.

American troops on the ground have complained in interviews that their intelligence officers underestimated both the numbers of the enemy and their combat skills. Pentagon officials deny this, saying it was impossible to gauge accurately the size of opposition forces that had been gathering in caves.

Reconnaissance forces slipped into the mountains a few days before the main attack was scheduled, but the operation was delayed a couple of days by bad weather. By Friday, March 1, the weather had cleared and at about 9 p.m. Eastern time — dawn in Afghanistan on Saturday — the offensive began.

"Early on, the situation changed pretty quickly," one senior officer said, referring to the Afghan retreat. "But in the main, the bad guys have gotten whipped badly."

— ERIC SCHMITT AND THOM SHANKER
MARCH 10, 2002

American troops arrive in a CH-47 "Chinook" helicopter on a hilltop in eastern Afghanistan. On March 2, American and coalition forces began a large-scale offensive against remaining Taliban and Al Qaeda forces. Near Sirkankel, Afghanistan. March 5, 2002.

POOL PHOTO BY WARREN ZINN

Perhaps someday there will be a reckoning for this tiny village of 15 houses, all of them obliterated into splintered wood and dust by American bombs. United States military officials might explain why 55 people died here.

But more likely, Madoo will not learn whether the bombs fell by mistake or on purpose, and the matter will be forgotten amid the larger consequences of war. It is left an anonymous hamlet with anonymous people buried in anonymous graves.

On December 1, American planes attacked several villages near the mountainous redoubt of Tora Bora in eastern Afghanistan, where Al Qaeda fighters—and perhaps even Osama bin Laden—were presumed to be hiding. It was an inauspicious beginning to a furious air campaign.

America's own anti-Taliban allies were horrified, claiming the targeting had been mistaken and that hundreds of innocents had been killed. It was "like a crime against humanity," said Hajji Muhammad Zaman, a military commander in the region. The Pentagon said little in response other than that it was sure of its quarry.

"Only Allah knows what has happened to us, and only Allah cares," said Abdul Hassain [a farmer walking through the hilltop cemetery].

"I blame the Arabs for this," said Paira Gul, his rage quieting as he grew used to his visitors. "The Arabs did not belong in Afghanistan, and it is because of them that the Americans have bombed." He considered his own appraisal of the situation, then amended his statement. "I blame both the Arabs and the Americans. They are all terrible people, the worst in all the world."

—**Barry Bearak**
december 16, 2001

Residents of Madoo stand amid the graves of 55 fellow civilians killed on December 1 when American bombs fell on the remote village. December 15, 2001.

An Afghan makes his way in a camp set up by the United Nations High Commissioner for Refugees in Chaman, Pakistan, about 500 yards from the Afghanistan border. October 24, 2001.

STRUGGLE FOR FOOD

Afghan refugees, past and present, "are people who have lost their land, their identities, their culture. For years, the nations of the world — Muslim or not — have been watching but not caring. Now they will pay the price. This generation of Afghans has already paid the price."

—TIM WEINER
quoting Fatana Ishaq Gailani, Director of the Afghanistan Women Council in Peshawar
NOVEMBER 26, 2001

*Three men guard American food packets dropped by planes overnight in
Afghanistan's Takhar province. October 13, 2001.*

Several wooden crates full of food, dropped by parachute, smashed
into at least four houses in this village on the edge of Herat, coming
through the roof in at least two instances. No one was injured. A
parachute and food crate also damaged a centuries-old shrine in
Herat where the Persian poet Khajeh Abdullah Ansari is buried,
according to photographers who visited the site.

Gholam Sedigh is an engineer who has been without work for
seven years. He does not know how he can afford to rebuild his
home, he said, and wants the Americans to compensate him. "They
should drop smaller packages, or they should drop nothing," he
said. "This is no less than a bomb."

Much of the food, which also included a melange of rice, pota-
toes, shortbread cookies, vegetable biscuits and strawberry jam,
had also opened and spilled upon impact. Some villagers wrinkled
their noses and said it smelled. "We're going to do a test and feed it
to the chickens first," teased Soltan Sabzehvari, 42, whose house
was also damaged.

But in a place where hunger is unyielding, there is a market for
the rations, at least those that landed intact. By this afternoon, the
food packets were selling, and selling well, for about 50 cents apiece
on the streets of Herat.

— **Amy Waldman**
NOVEMBER 21, 2001

Afghan refugees make their new home at the interim camp set up by the United Nations High Commissioner for Refugees. Chaman, Pakistan. October 24, 2001.

Fazal Muhammed, 42, lost his right middle finger to a mine two years ago. In October 2001, he lost the sight in his left eye and his 5-year-old son, Taj, when two U.S. bombs struck a munitions facility one kilometer from his home, in the village of Lowall, outside of Kandahar, Afghanistan. Quetta, Pakistan. October 14, 2001.

Zibida, 10, stands among the women as they wait for food distribution. It is the first food distributed to refugees since bombing began in the Kunduz district. Bagh-i-Shirkat refugee camp, Afghanistan. December 10, 2001.

CHANG W. LEE/NYT

IN THE CAMPS

The retreat of the Taliban has opened the next critical phase of the American campaign in Afghanistan: joining the effort to deliver relief for millions of hungry, cold, sick, war-weary Afghans, thousands of them at death's door. In the end, the war against famine, disease and misery may prove as important as the military campaign in ending a generation of misrule and chaos.

The military will be full partners in the mobilization now getting under way. NATO allies will ship food, clothing, shelter and medicine to the nations surrounding Afghanistan for United Nations relief organizations, private aid groups and intrepid Afghan truckers to deliver to people in ruined cities and shattered villages. The United States is buying millions of tons of wheat, much of it delivered in red, white and blue bags stamped USA, to help keep Afghans from starving this winter.

This is not pure charity. It is basic strategy, part of the West's campaign to show Afghans that the American-led coalition can help them live new lives.

"I saw a family on the way, a husband, a pregnant wife, carrying two small children and their belongings," said Tilawat Shah, 32, who arrived alone from Jalalabad. "They could carry them no longer. They kissed their children and left them in the mountains."

—TIM WEINER
NOVEMBER 16, 2001

Shamali refugees have been living in the ruins of the Soviet Embassy
in Kabul for several years. January 2, 2002.

A Pakistani girl at the Punj Puti refugee camp. Quetta, Pakistan. November 11, 2001.

REFUGEES

Those fleeing war joined those fleeing hunger, and there were those, the double-damned, who fled both. By late 2000, there was a crisis of displaced people, some of them escaping Afghanistan, some just escaping their villages.

—TIM WEINER
NOVEMBER 16, 2001

Abandoned

The Afghanistan the Taliban left behind is a sad and broken land. To a visitor, the country seems an almost apocalyptic place, scattered with ruins and orphans and the detritus of wars.

In the five years that the Taliban held the capital, their record as a government might be measured by the numbers they produced: nearly one million refugees, joining the million others who had already left and refused to come home; six million Afghans, a quarter of the country, unable to find enough food.

But the real legacy of the Taliban rule lies deeper and is harder to grasp. A journey around Afghanistan, beginning on the border with Tajikistan and ending 400 miles away in Kandahar, revealed deep psychological wounds in a people still struggling with the torment of a government regarded by many as oppressive and strange.

—**Dexter Filkins**
DECEMBER 31, 2001

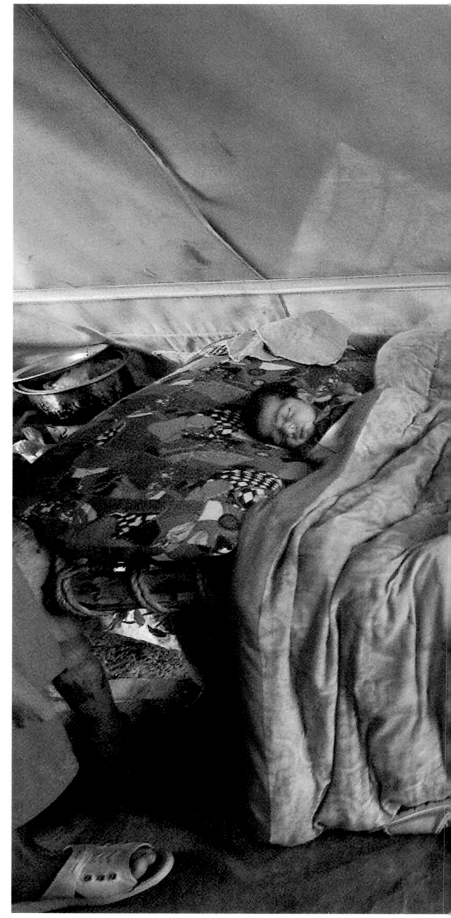

With her newborn daughter sleeping at left, Malika, a refugee from a village near Jalalabad, Afghanistan, looks out of a tent in the New Shamshatoo Refugee Camp in Pakistan. October 16, 2001.

THE CHALLENGE ABROAD
199

After the first harsh blasts of winter, half a million or more people are homeless and half-starved inside Afghanistan. The United Nations says 130,000 refugees have come to Pakistan since the American bombing started in early October. Tens of thousands are shivering through the night in refugee camps. With Taliban control slipping in the south, the United Nations' refugee agency said it is worried about a new influx into Pakistan, and rushed to send more tents and blankets to the borders.

—TIM WEINER
NOVEMBER 16, 2001

A refugee stands by his tent in a camp on the outskirts of Mazar-i-Sharif as the first snow of winter falls. The refugees fled fighting between the Northern Alliance and Taliban forces. December 3, 2001.

JAMES HILL FOR NYT

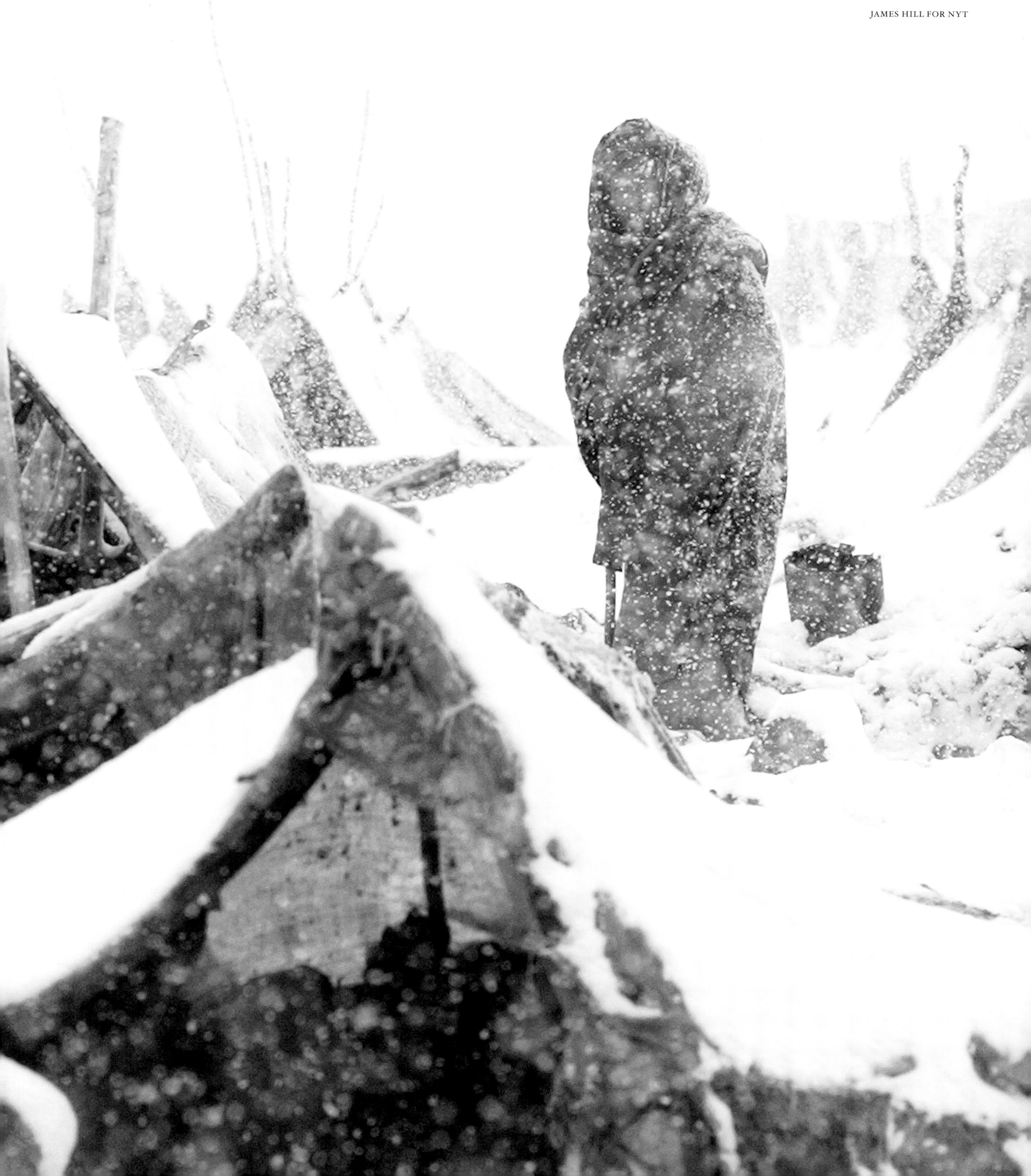

THE LIBERATION OF KABUL

Three weeks after the Taliban's exodus from Kabul, people are cauterizing the psychic wounds left by the religious police and resuming those parts of their lives outlawed by an uncompromising vision of Islamic purity.

Joy may be too strong a word for the common mood in Afghanistan's capital, for there is wariness of the future. The nation is once again riven into fiefs under the control of tribal chiefs and brutal warlords. What peace there is seems threadbare. But surely, at least for now, a shared sense of relief has embraced the city.

Gone are not only the Taliban but also the horrific American bombing raids that were meant to subdue them. There is fresh wreckage, though a guide is needed to locate it. Kabul was already a violated city.

Indeed, the essential look of the mountain-ringed city remains the same. Cars still maneuver around the pushcarts and donkey-led wagons. Withered old men carry bundles of firewood strapped to their shoulders. Shrouded women move through the bazaars like downtrodden ghosts. Children use the remnants of collapsed buildings as playgrounds.

Only with a second look come the sights that would have been unthinkable a month ago. Over there, some men are clean-shaven, the hat of the Northern Alliance substituting for the turbans preferred by the Taliban. Over here are a few courageous women, walking outdoors without the head-to-toe burka.

—**BARRY BEARAK**
DECEMBER 2, 2001

A tank crowded with Northern Alliance troops rumbles into Kabul after the Taliban fled the city. November 13, 2001.

KOJI HARADA/KYODO VIA REUTERS

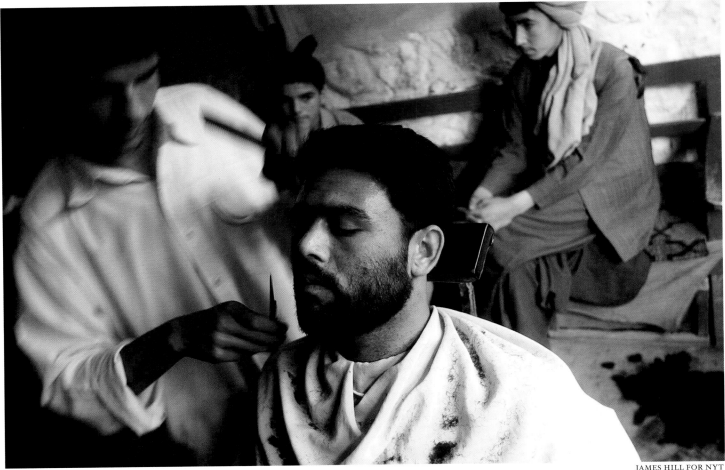

Mohammad Hassan, 22, gets his beard cut at the barber's shop the day after his city's liberation by Northern Alliance forces. Taloqan, Afghanistan. November 12, 2001.

A New Way of Life

Men gather at a Kabul market to watch a quail fight, which along with other, more intense blood sports had long been banned by the Taliban. Betting on quail or gamecocks is again the rage in the capital, and organized dogfights are planned for the spring. December 1, 2001.

Residents of several cities in Afghanistan greeted fighters last week from the opposition Northern Alliance, showering them with flowers and money in some places, and celebrating in a variety of ways.

The Taliban imposed a harsh variety of Islam that brought them condemnation around the globe. All men had to wear beards at least four inches long. No woman could work or go to school or leave the house alone, and women had to be completely covered if they ventured out of their houses at all. Television and music and many other forms of recreation were banned.

Last week, men in the liberated cities had their beards trimmed. Women uncovered their faces and walked freely out of doors. People listened to music and brought their television sets out of hiding.

NOVEMBER 18, 2001

Afghan men on horseback "playing" buzkashi, a contest in which a participant wins by being the one to place a dead goat or calf carcass in a circle. Kabul, Afghanistan. December 28, 2001.

CHILDREN IN A HARSH LAND

His face was dirty and his pants, cinched tight with rope, were several inches too wide in the waist. His rubber boots looked twice the size of his feet. He is 8 years old and has never been to school. He reached into his sweater, pulled out a few pages of Arabic script and began to read.

It was not much, merely the alphabet in Dari, but in Afghanistan it is enough to move him well ahead of his peers. He lowered the grubby book and smiled.

[The children] are a huge mass of people, largely illiterate and mostly unvaccinated — some skilled in the basics of waging war, others without any moral reference point after being raised under the Taliban's brand of law.

They are savvy to the streets and the steppe, yet without the slightest sense of the world. Here one can meet 10-year-old boys who can clean a carburetor, butcher a sheep, point out a land mine, disassemble a Russian rifle or look after a storekeeper's stall.

There are also unsettling signs in children who have been exposed to so much violence and severity that they have little sense of their meaning. Mirwais, a 12-year-old boy in Kunduz, said that earlier this year he stood in a crowd on the city's main soccer field and watched the Taliban lop a hand and a foot from each of two men accused of theft.

He saw nothing odd about it. He thought it strange that someone would ask. "They were criminal people," he said. "That is what criminal people get."

At the moment, the efforts to help children are patchwork and informal.

—**C.J. Chivers**
DECEMBER 4, 2001

Top: Ambrook, 6, in white hat, and his brother Baryallai carry water to place in a donkey's basket. Alchin, Afghanistan. Middle: Mill Agha, 10, left, Habibulah, 7, and Jamila, 5, right, who are siblings, earn up to $2 a day working as porters. Kabul, Afghanistan. Bottom: Children at play. Kunduz, Afghanistan. December 23, 2001.

PHOTOGRAPHS BY CHANG W. LEE/NYT

While relatives watched, Afghan children rode an improvised carousel that had been made from artillery shell casings. Rides cost 5,000 Afghanis, or about 10 cents. Mazar-i-Sharif. December 15, 2001.

CHILDREN AS BARTER

Haunted by want, depleted from hunger, Akhtar Muhammad first sold off his few farm animals and then, as the months passed, bartered away the family's threadbare rugs and its metal cooking utensils and even some of the wooden beams that held up the hard-packed roof of his overcrowded hovel.

But always the hunger outlasted the money. And finally, six weeks ago, Mr. Muhammad did something that has become ruefully unremarkable in this desperate country. He took two of his 10 children to the bazaar of the nearest city and traded them for bags of wheat.

Gone now from his home are the boys, Sher, 10, and Baz, 5. "What else could I do?" the bereft father asked today in Kangori, a remote hamlet in the mountains of northern Afghanistan. He did not want to seem uncaring. "I miss my sons, but there was nothing to eat," he said, casting a glance sideways to prove that his misery was hardly unusual.

In the nearby foothills, enfeebled people were coming back from foraging wild spinach and even blades of grass — a harvest of hideously bitter greenery that can be made edible only if boiled long enough. "For some, there is nothing else," Mr. Muhammad muttered.

In Afghanistan, two decades of war have also left it hard to distinguish between the bad times and the worse. Even without famine, more than one in five children die before the age of 5 and the average life expectancy is a mere 44.

These days, food is a lodestone, luring the hungry from their homes and into huge camps where paltry monthly rations — usually just one hefty sack of wheat per family — are nevertheless dependably supplied.

"The key word is return," said Mireille Borne of the aid group Acted. "If you just give away food, you undermine the economy. You have to think about the long term."

The long term is what most disconsolate parents are thinking of when they sell their children. There is not much precedent in Afghanistan for this heart-wrenching sacrifice. Traditionally, girls are "sold" for marriage, with the bride's family collecting a price.

But what is occurring now is closer to the practice of bonded labor. Arrangements differ but most often the child is exchanged for a continuing supply of cash or wheat.

"The family was very hungry and I needed help in my restaurant," said Muhammad Aslam, explaining why he bought two young brothers nearly two years ago. As he sipped tea, Bashir, 13, and Qadir, 11, were cleaning the cooking area in the narrow establishment in Sholgarah. "It is cheaper to buy boys than hire boys. Actually, I could have had them free."

Mr. Aslam described the transaction: the boys' father had offered to give up his sons so long as they were kept well fed. "But I know about human rights," said the restaurant owner. "I knew I was obligated to pay him something."

The compensation settled upon was 400,000 Afghanis per month — about $5 at the time of the deal. "After two years, I stop paying and the boys are mine forever," Mr. Aslam said happily, presenting the situation as something as benevolent as an adoption.

He asked the youngsters to sit at his side. He requested a smile. They complied.

Abdul Hamid, a porter, was also seated in the restaurant. "I've bought three children, all from different families," he volunteered. Noor Agha is 8, Amruddin 9, Malik 11. He sent someone to get the boys. He said he considered himself a doer of good deeds.

"These families were all hungry," Mr. Hamid said. "They cannot give their children what I can. The boys work for me, but I also send them to school. They are becoming my sons. If they get lonely, I have agreed to let them see their real parents every six months."

Akhtar Muhammad, with his family starving in Kangori, bargained harder than most. For his 10-year-old, Sher, he now receives a stipend of 46 pounds of wheat per month; for the younger boy, 5-year-old Baz, he receives half that amount. The deal continues for six years.

"I have sold the two most intelligent of my 10 children," the father said insistently.

Akhtar Muhammad with his son, Sher, 10, whom he sold for 46 pounds of wheat a month. Angori, Afghanistan. March 2, 2002.

Six weeks had passed since his sons were delivered to Sholgarah. He agreed to ride into the town, to search out his older boy, to inquire about the lad's uprooted life.

By chance, father and son happened upon each other in a crowded street. Immediately, they embraced. Sher was astride a donkey, toting several metal jugs. He had been sent to fetch a supply of water.

"They don't treat me well," the boy said sorrowfully when asked. Indeed, looking away from his father, his eyes moistened. He seemed close to sobbing.

"I work very hard and during the night they send me into the mountains to sleep with the sheep."

His father listened silently with no telling expression on his face. "I felt bad that I was sold," the boy continued, staring down now, swallowing his shame. "I cried. Sometimes I still cry. I cry at night. But I understand why the selling of me was necessary."

He is his family's antidote to hunger.

"I must go now," the 10-year-old said, riding off. "I must hurry or they will beat me."

—— **BARRY BEARAK**
MARCH 8, 2002

At School

Haziza, a 12-year-old refugee from Afghanistan, sits in a row alone in a first grade classroom with children much younger than she is. They raise their hands to answer a question she can't. Under Taliban rule in Afghanistan, Haziza was not allowed to go to school and now, in Pakistan, she is struggling to make up for missed years of education. Peshawar, Pakistan. October 26, 2001.

RUTH FREMSON/NYT

At the Ariana School here in Peshawar, the newly arrived students — the Afghans who have fled the American bombs — are easy to detect. They are anxious. They are mournful. They are withdrawn. And also, they are a head taller than the others in class.

As the new children at Ariana tell their stories, rueful themes repeat: the pummeling fury of the air raids, the uncoupling from all that is familiar, the exhausting journey over the mountains, the unremitting neediness of the refugee life.

The years of Taliban rule have not only denied girls an education but boys as well. Their schools may have been open but very little teaching was going on. And when teaching did occur, religion very often replaced reading, writing and arithmetic in the curriculum.

— **BARRY BEARAK**
OCTOBER 30, 2001

VINCENT LAFORET/NYT

Young girls study at a midrasa in the Khursan refugee camp near Peshawar, Pakistan, right. September 28, 2001. Young boys do likewise at a midrasa in Akora Khattak, Pakistan, left. September 17, 2001. The midrasas provide free education to youngsters, sometimes the only education they will receive. Midrasas are sometimes accused of being breeding grounds for Islamic extremists.

BEHIND THE BURKA

Sima Rezahi, 22, hopes to work to support her elderly parents. Her sister Zahra, 17, left their family's house yesterday for the first time in two years but was afraid to be photographed without a burka. Herat, Afghanistan. November 18, 2001.

In the walled garden of her house, Soheila Helal waged a quiet rebellion against the Taliban. On a patio softened by rugs and book-ended by two small blackboards, she ran a school for 120 students, mostly girls. It was a transgression on two counts: as a woman Mrs. Helal was not supposed to work, and her female students were not supposed to learn.

So her students' lessons included what to tell any Taliban forces who stopped them — that they were just going to visit her. The after-school activities included learning how to leave discreetly in small groups, so as not to attract attention.

"I thought of killing myself many times," she said of life under the Taliban.

The freedom is still too new to completely trust, and the wounds too fresh to be healed, but for the first time in years, women here say they have hope — that they will be treated like human beings, not wayward cattle; that they will be free to leave their homes and work; that their daughters will be able to learn.

Today women showed off bruises and scars earned for going it alone or daring to speak in a government office. They described the cruel illogic of the Taliban: male doctors were not allowed to treat women but female doctors were not permitted to be trained; many widows here who were the sole support of their family were barred from going to work. Many of them resorted to shelling nuts or washing clothes at home, barely earning enough to fill their children's stomachs.

Women also showed resilience, even crafty defiance, for those who were expected to be neither seen nor heard. Knowing they would be lashed, they went out alone anyway. Confined to their homes, many taught their daughters to read. They started secret schools or secured small concessions — permission to open a nursing school, for example — from the Taliban bureaucracy.

—AMY WALDMAN
NOVEMBER 19, 2001

Jamillah, who fled the drought in Afghanistan, holds her 10-month-old son, Shabanah, at the Doctors Without Borders clinic in the Jalozi refugee camp. Peshawar, Pakistan. November 6, 2001.

The Smugglers

The smugglers come down from the mountains each morning at sunrise, their donkeys in tow, laden with rice and tea and cooking oil.

These days, the smugglers are returning with stories as well: of beatings and shootings at the hands of Taliban guards, of bribes and detentions and arrests. Of old routes blocked, goods seized and friends taken away.

In the five years that this mountainous swath of northern Afghanistan has held out against the Taliban, smuggling has been the trade that has kept it alive. With the country's northern border with Tajikistan mostly sealed, the secret routes into Taliban-controlled territory have supplied Afghans on the rebel side with almost every conceivable need: food, soap, clothing, even weapons. The trade has continued through the worst of times — slowing during heavy fighting, but nearly always carrying on through the mountain passes and valley roads that crisscross this desolate landscape.

Now, the rules have changed. The smugglers who gather in border towns like this one say that the Taliban soldiers who guard the trade routes, and who even a few weeks ago allowed the commerce to pass without much trouble, are now edgy and violent, accusing the smugglers of aiding their enemies, the Northern Alliance and the United States. The smugglers who have made it safely back say they are paying a higher price for their efforts, in steeper bribes and sometimes with beatings and death.

—Dexter Filkins
October 26, 2001

A smuggler with his donkeys. Fakhar, Afghanistan. October 25, 2001.

THE CHALLENGE ABROAD

ETHNIC LINES

In the villages that mark the barren landscape, Afghanistan's myriad ethnic groups live mostly peaceably together, often sharing power, swapping languages and blurring ethnic lines in their choice of marriage partners.

But the region's newcomers, usually refugees and soldiers from other parts, often hold a different view. As those who have experienced the ethnically drawn fighting that has come to mark Afghanistan's civil war, they increasingly see their country, and themselves, through the prism of their own ethnic identities. Many of them say they would find it difficult to put aside their grievances and reach across ethnic lines and work together in a new government if the country's civil war ever came to an end.

"The Pashtuns have committed so many crimes," said Habibullah, an Uzbek refugee in the town of Khwaja Bahaouddin. "How can we work with them after this?"

— **DEXTER FILKINS**
NOVEMBER 3, 2001

AFGHANISTAN'S ETHNIC GROUPS

Afghanistan's ethnic groups figure prominently in the country's civil war. Maps show where each group is predominant.

Pashtun

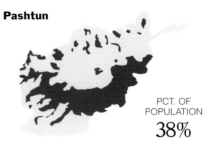

PCT. OF POPULATION
38%

The Pashtuns make up an over-whelming majority of the Taliban.

Tajik

PCT. OF POPULATION
25%

The Tajiks make up a majority of the force fighting the Taliban.

Hazara

PCT. OF POPULATION
19%

Many Hazaras, a religious minority, are opposed to the Taliban.

Turkmen

PCT. OF POPULATION
LESS THAN **10%**

An ethnic minority, Turkmens mainly side with the Northern Alliance.

Uzbek

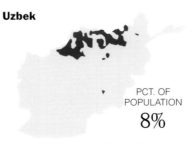

PCT. OF POPULATION
8%

Many rally around Abdul Rashid Dostum, a warlord fighting the Taliban.

Source: Central Intelligence Agency   THE NEW YORK TIMES

Pashtuns, Uzbeks, Tajiks and Hazaras gather to celebrate the engagement of a Pashtun couple. Pashtun, Afghanistan. October 28, 2001.

OPIUM

The Taliban are gone from here. So is their ban on growing opium poppies. Afghanistan's production of raw opium fell from a world-record peak of more than a million pounds in 1999 to a mere 40,600 pounds this year, a 96 percent decline, according to the United Nations Drug Control Program.

Say what one will about the Taliban, they just said no to poppies, imprisoning farmers who defied them. But now, barring an unexpected turn of events, Afghanistan can be expected to regain its status as the world's leading source of heroin in a year or two.

—TIM WEINER
NOVEMBER 26, 2001

Muhammad Tahir is from the village of Gudara, population perhaps 4,000.

"We are poor people," Mr. Tahir said only 30 hours before the last bombs fell. "Our trees are our only shelter from the cold and wind. The trees have been bombed. Our waterfall, our only source of water — they bombed it. Where is the humanity?

"Civilized countries talk about human rights and then they bomb us. Give my message to the Pentagon: This is our village. This is our only place for living."

Timur Shah is a farmer, 27, blind in one eye, missing his right leg. A Soviet mine blew them away when he was 14.

"In Taliban time there was peace. But the Taliban were only concerned with law and order, the beard and the turban. They were not concerned with jobs and industry, nothing else. We expect this new regime to create jobs here and all over Afghanistan.

"Now if someone asks us to quit growing poppy, we can — if there are jobs," he added. "We feel guilty about it, but there is no other way.

"I know the poppy is poison for everyone. But are you ready to tell me not to cultivate it? We will die from lack of bread and food."

—TIM WEINER
DECEMBER 3, 2001

PHOTOGRAPHS BY VINCENT LAFORET/NYT

A man struggles to keep his eyes open after inhaling opium, as fellow addicts jokingly prop a snake on his head. Quetta, Pakistan. September 30, 2001.

Opium addicts light up inside a cave at Quetta Satellite Cemetery. September 30, 2001.

STREET PORTRAITS

PHOTOGRAPHS BY STEPHEN CROWLEY/NYT

ZAHIR SHAH, 24 "I have my own little bit of land. I raise corn and vegetables, and I have four sheep and six cows. This is my bird. When I run out of money I take one and come to the city and sell it at the bazaar. I heard last night on the BBC's Pashto Service that there is a harvest festival and they eat this bird. We call it elephant bird."

The story of Afghanistan is like Job's, except God has not yet appeared in the whirlwind to explain the suffering and set things right. This is a land where war has put time out of joint, where people live in ruins resembling archaeological sites, using the tools of centuries gone by. The tools — hand-hewn wooden furrows plowing the earth, hand-shaped clay ovens baking bread — create the beautiful necessities that make life bearable.

Using the type of camera operated by street photographers in Afghanistan to provide photographs for visas and passports, we recorded the faces of the Afghan people in the market town of Jalalabad, Afghanistan, about 20 miles south of Tora Bora. The handmade camera and the methods used are the same technology photographers used at the turn of the 20th century. The lens has no shutter. Instead, the two- to six-second exposures are made by manipulating the lens cover. The image is exposed on photosensitive paper rather than film. This simple camera captured the fetid, dusty air of the bazaar and the simple ways of the culture in a way that color could not.

We stopped passers-by at random in late November — street urchins, ragpickers, farmers, tradesmen, freelance gunmen — all shattered by fighting and praying for peace. We took their portraits and spoke with them while the negatives developed. The negatives were photographed with a digital camera and transformed into positive images in a laptop computer.

It was Ramazan, a man with the eyes of the ancient mariner, who told us how war had torn Afghanistan. When he was young, he said, his village was a paradise of orchards and roses, a peaceable kingdom. Now they are gone, he said, and "we don't know what the weather is or what the seasons are."

—TIM WEINER AND STEPHEN CROWLEY
MARCH 27, 2002

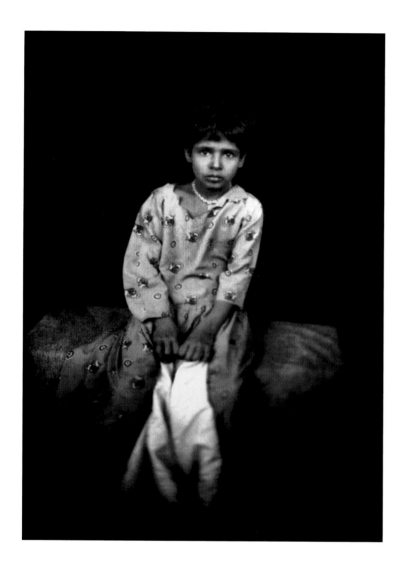 

BREAKHNA, 9 Her name means lightning. "I love school but I have no money to buy books and go to school now. I pick garbage. I get plastic. It's useful. I walk an hour from my home to go work. I have heard the noises of the bombs at night. I start crying, my mother hugs me, but I can't sleep."

ROMEL, 13 He is a seventh-grade student. "I saw my cousin killed from the bombing. He was 20. His name was Muhammad Afzal. I don't want to remember that scene. There has been a lot of bombing near my village in the last two months. A lot of houses destroyed. A lot of killing of innocent people. That is our luck. If there is fighting among Arabs, Taliban and America, why do they hit civilians? We didn't do anything."

ABDUL HAQ (does not know his age) "My father was killed in the fighting years ago and we had no money so I started working for my uncle, who stitches shoes. Last year I got my own shoeshine box and polish and started working. I get three Pakistani rupees a shine [about 5 cents]. I don't have money for school, so I work. I would love to go. When the bombing started, almost everyone on my street ran away, some to Pakistan, some far away. That was my nightmare night."

ROHEEL (thinks he is 10) He sells bolani, a savory bread, for about 4 cents apiece. "When I grow up I want to be a doctor. Because in this city we need doctors. There are many injured people here, because there is fighting."

RAMAZAN, 42 He is a barber from the village of Karghi, in Laghman province. "I lost my four young ones in the bombardment one month ago. Javaid was 7 years old, Zamoor was 6, Hidayat was 4 and Mushabana was 1 1/2. In the time of King Zahir Shah, I was a young man, about 16. There was no pain at that time. There was freedom then. We felt the seasons, summer changing into winter. Now, the last 23 years, we don't know what the weather is or what the seasons are. If God wills it, it may once again be like it was. But I'm not sure."

AHMAD FAWAD, 18 "I'm from Kabul. I heard the news that there was peace in Jalalabad and I came looking for work. I'm a carpenter. My father was a carpenter too. Almost all the homes where I live were destroyed starting when I was about 10 years old. It was Hekmatyar, who became prime minister. First he destroys the houses, then he destroys the city, then he became prime minister. That's how it goes here. I have not seen peace in my whole life. From childhood, I have seen blood, bullets, guns, nothing else. If there is peace, and they want me to build houses, I'm ready to work night and day."

DANIEL PEARL
1963-2002

"I promise you that the terrorists did not defeat my husband no matter what they did to him, nor did they succeed in seizing his dignity or value as a human being."

—MARIANE PEARL
FEBRUARY 23, 2002

Colleagues and friends said that the work the 38-year-old Mr. Pearl left behind shows where his talents lay: in doggedly pursuing and explaining obscure topics, or superficially simple ones, with sensitivity and nuance. He saw that as his mission, friends said, and he died pursuing it.

—SUSAN SAULNY
FEBRUARY 22, 2002

Three days after Mr. Pearl failed to return home from his evening meeting, Pakistani and Western news organizations received an e-mail message accompanied by the pictures shown above. On January 30, a second e-mail message said he would be killed if the kidnappers' demands — including a repatriation of the Pakistani prisoners now in American custody in Cuba — were not met within 24 hours.

Daniel Pearl, the Wall Street Journal reporter abducted in Pakistan four weeks ago, has been killed by his captors, according to Pakistani and United States officials. A videotape delivered to Pakistani officials late Wednesday and now in the possession of F.B.I. agents gives unambiguous proof of his death, officials said.

The delivery of the cassette ended a month of uncertainty punctuated by unfounded reports of Mr. Pearl's condition and the likelihood of his safe return. These lent the investigation an air of confusion and also whipsawed the emotions of his wife, Mariane, who is pregnant, his parents and his colleagues.

The case of Mr. Pearl, who was 38 and had been The Journal's South Asia bureau chief for about two years, had been the subject of high-level attention by American and Pakistani officials, and Mr. Pearl's death seemed likely to prompt new American pressure on Pakistan to crack down on the Islamic militants believed to have carried out the crime.

His killing appears to have been intended as part of a campaign of retaliation by Pakistani militants against President Pervez Musharraf, who has turned his back on the Taliban and on other extremists who have long had ties with the Pakistani government. It also served as an affront to General Musharraf's prestige, since his government had expressed optimism that the case would be solved and Mr. Pearl returned unharmed.

As the war in Afghanistan wound down, Mr. Pearl, who was known among colleagues in the region as a cautious reporter, began to investigate the case of Richard C. Reid, who has been accused of plotting to destroy a Paris-to-Miami passenger jet with explosives hidden in his shoe.

Mr. Reid, a British citizen, had studied Islam in Pakistan, reportedly with a figure named Sheik Gilani. Mr. Pearl was seeking to meet with Sheik Gilani when he began telephone and e-mail negotiations that led him to a Karachi restaurant called The Village, where he was apparently met by his abductors.

Shortly after the abduction, which took place on January 23, the kidnappers began communicating through e-mail messages whose tone was stridently anti-American. They accused Mr. Pearl of being an agent of first the C.I.A. and then the Mossad, the Israeli intelligence agency. The second verified e-mail transmission also contained a message in Urdu. As translated by The New York Times, it began, "Our intention is not to harm Pakistan but to rid it of the slavery of America and other countries."

Among the steps American officials are said to be considering is a request to Pakistan to extradite the prime suspect in the case to the United States for trial. The suspect, Ahmed Omar Sheikh, is a British-born militant who told a Pakistani court that he had been involved in the crime.

— **FELICITY BARRINGER WITH DOUGLAS JEHL**
FEBRUARY 22, 2002

Pakistani police with Fahad Naseem, accused of acting as an accomplice to Ahmed Omar Saeed Sheikh in the Pearl kidnapping and murder. Karachi, Pakistan. February 21, 2002.

AAMIR QURESHI/AGENCE FRANCE-PRESSE

THREAT OF THE WARLORDS

The galaxy of warlords who tore Afghanistan apart in the early 1990's and who were vanquished by the Taliban because of their corruption and perfidy are back on their thrones, poised to exercise power in the ways they always have.

From the western part of the country to the east, control of the strategic cities passed in less than a week to the same warlords who fled from the Taliban up to six years ago.

Even in Kandahar, the last city still held by the Taliban, the ruler who handed the city over to the Taliban — Mullah Naquib — has been designated as a possible successor to the Taliban leader, Mullah Muhammad Omar.

The rapid return of the warlords will make the task of forming the broad-based Afghan government the Bush administration says it wants to help forge much more difficult.

Since possession of territory is the most important facet of political power in Afghanistan, the warlords are in no hurry to form coalitions, he said. Most of the big warlords are affiliated with the Northern Alliance, whose commanders in Kabul are refusing to remove their troops, an important first step if negotiations for a new government embracing all of the country's factions are to get under way.

Mr. Rashid said that in order to help bring order to the chaos, some kind of international force needed to be deployed throughout Afghanistan, and the major Western powers needed to send diplomats to help push the political process along.

—JANE PERLEZ
NOVEMBER 19, 2001

The soldiers of a defeated warlord, Padsha Khan Zadran, were held in a dungeon by the soldiers of a rival commander, Saifullah, in Gardez, Afghanistan, after a two-day battle. January 31, 2002.

THE CHALLENGE ABROAD

227

THE NEW HOPE

Hamid Karzai, who has been named to lead an interim govern-ment in Afghanistan, is at once a traditional tribal chief from the Taliban stronghold of Kandahar and a longtime anti-Taliban leader who became known to policy makers in Washington.

Since slipping into southern Afghanistan from [Pakistan] in October, Mr. Karzai has represented the main American hope for a southern resistance, as he traveled from town to town and persuaded fellow Pashtun leaders to turn against the Taliban.

After narrowly escaping death last month, apparently thanks to an American military helicopter, Mr. Karzai stood tonight some 10 miles north of Kandahar, which remained under the control of Mullah Muhammad Omar and Arab fighters.

"My priorities are to work for the peace and security of Afghanistan," Mr. Karzai said tonight by satellite telephone.

—**NORIMITSU ONISHI**
DECEMBER 6, 2001

Hamid Karzai, the leader of Afghanistan's new interim government, after his inauguration ceremony in the capital. December 22, 2001.

THE CHALLENGE ABROAD

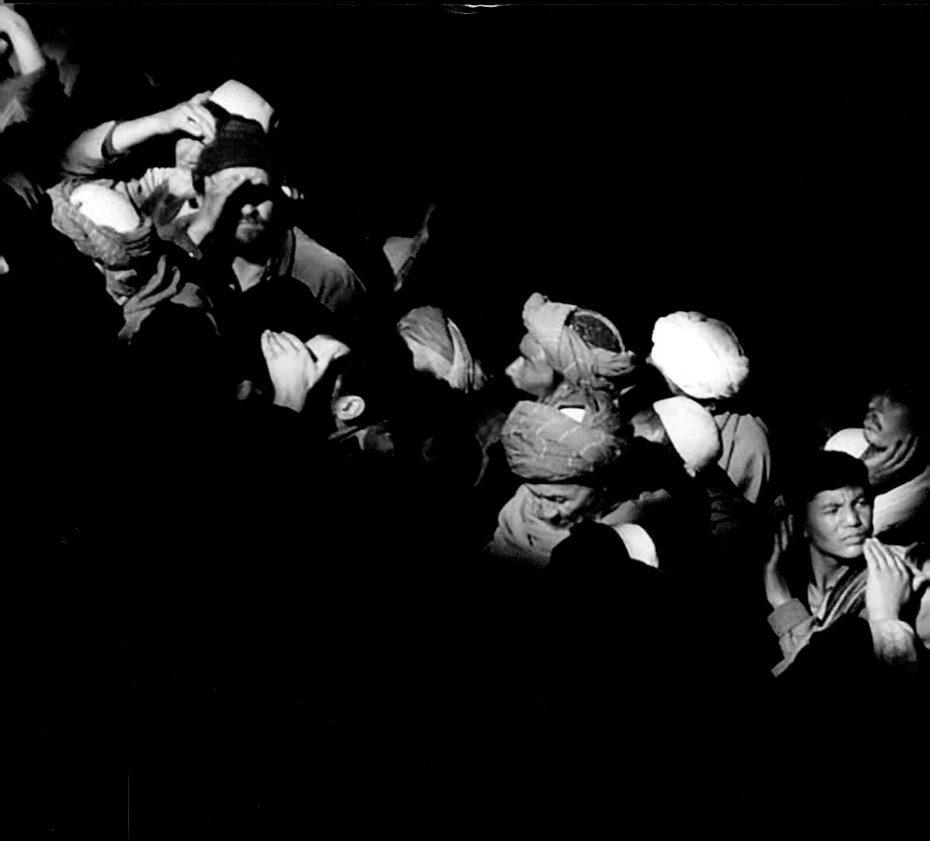

Hazara people try to block the sunlight during the welcoming ceremony of their returning leader Karim Khalili at Mohamadia Mosque in Kartasaki town. Mr. Khalili returned to Kabul after five years of fighting the Taliban. December 27, 2001.

THE DOVES ARE BACK

Few people here profess to know what the future will bring to Mazar-i-Sharif, or Afghanistan, but for now, the omens seem good.

At the Azrat Ali mosque, the doves have returned. The birds are a famous part of this city: according to legend the birds were brought by Sultan Hussein Baiqhra in the 17th century from Nejev in modern-day Iraq. Nejev is said to hold the body of Ali, the son of Islam's Holy Prophet, Muhammad, and Mazar-i-Sharif, his spirit.

Quri Amonullah, the mullah at Azrat Ali, said the doves were the first to leave when the fighting started in Mazar-i-Sharif, and often the last to return.

"They went to special hiding places," the turbaned cleric said. "Sometimes for many days."

But now the doves that have seen so much seem to be sticking around.

—**DEXTER FILKINS**
DECEMBER 9, 2001

At the shrine of Azrat Ali in Mazar-i-Sharif, the mosque's mullah says the doves are the first to leave when fighting breaks out and the last to return. December 6, 2001.

JAMES HILL FOR NYT

THE CHALLENGE ABROAD

233

ALMANAC OF TERROR

SELECTED FACTS AND FIGURES

THE ATTACK

- 8:46:26 a.m.: American Airlines Flight 11, a Boeing 767, scheduled to fly from Boston to Los Angeles, hits the north tower of the World Trade Center in lower Manhattan.

- Flight 11 carried 10,000 gallons of jet fuel and was traveling at an estimated 586 miles per hour. It slammed into the north tower between the 94th and 98th floors, exploding with the force of 480,000 pounds of dynamite. The blast registered on the Lamont Observatory seismograph, 21 miles north of Manhattan, at a magnitude of 0.9 — equal to a small earth tremor.

- 9:02:54 a.m.: United Airlines Flight 175, a Boeing 767, scheduled to fly from Boston to Los Angeles, hits the south tower of the World Trade Center.

- Flight 175, traveling about 480 miles per hour and also heavily laden with fuel, struck the south tower between the 78th and 84th floors.

- 9:38 a.m.: American Airlines Flight 77, a Boeing 757, scheduled to fly from Washington, D.C., to Los Angeles, hits the Pentagon.

- 9:59:04 a.m.: The south tower collapses.

- 10:06 a.m.: United Airlines Flight 93, a Boeing 757 scheduled to fly from Newark, New Jersey, to San Francisco, crashes 80 miles southeast of Pittsburgh.

- 10:28:31 a.m. The north tower of the World Trade Center collapses, registering 2.3 on the magnitude scale at the seismograph at Lamont Observatory.

- All 246 passengers and crew on the four planes die, as do the 19 Arab hijackers, all of whom are members of Al Qaeda, the terrorist group headed by Osama bin Laden. Fifteen of the 19 were, like Mr. bin Laden, Saudi Arabians.

- On an average workday, 35,000 people were in the World Trade Center towers by 9 a.m. On September 11, each tower held between 5,000 and 7,000 people.

- As of April 22, 2002, 2,825 people, from more than 115 countries, were listed as having died in the attacks on the World Trade Center. On September 24, the New York Police Department had estimated that the death toll could be as high as 6,659.

Among the dead were:
- 343 firefighters and paramedics
- 23 New York Police Department officers
- 37 Port Authority police officers
- 658 employees of the bond trading firm of Cantor Fitzgerald, located on four floors in the north tower.

- 78 employees of Windows on the World, the restaurant on the 106th floor of the north tower.

- 147 dead on two hijacked planes
- 134 missing
- 934 death certificates issued by medical examiner's office
- 1,759 death certificates issued at request of families in cases in which remains have not been identified

- Based on an analysis of death certificates for more than 90 percent of the estimated 2,825 World Trade Center victims, three times as many men as women died; the greatest number of those who died were between the ages of 35 and 39. Victims were residents of at least 25 states, with 64 percent coming from New York State. The youngest victim appears to be Christine Lee Hanson of Groton, Massachusetts, who was 2 1/2 years old and a passenger on Flight 175. The oldest victim apparently was Robert Grant Norton, 85, of Lubec, Maine and a passenger on Flight 11.

- 184 people died at the Pentagon, with 59 dead on the hijacked plane.

- In Pennsylvania, 40 people died on the hijacked plane.

- Cleanup of the site began almost immediately, and operated 24 hours a day, seven days a week. At any given time, 600 to 700 people worked at the site. As of April 8, 2002, 101,759 truckloads of debris, weighing 1,506,124 tons, had been removed, including 183,863 tons of steel.

- The cost of the cleanup will be about $600 million, well below previous estimates of $2 billion. Cleanup should be completed in May or June 2002; original estimates had been two to three years.

- $230 million in gold and silver (379,036 troy ounces of gold and 29,942,619 million troy ounces of silver) belonging to the Bank of Nova Scotia were buried in a vault under 4 World Trade Center. Removal began in March 2002 under armed guard.

- A secret C.I.A. station was buried under 7 World Trade Center, which collapsed several hours after the towers. The undercover office, disguised behind a false front using the name of another federal organization, was a base for operations aimed at spying on and recruiting foreign diplomats.

- More than 30 major charities have collected at least $1.4 billion in aid for the families of the victims of September 11. As of March 11, 2002, the Red Cross had raised $930 million to aid September 11 victims, and had distributed $558 million.

• • •

- The World Trade Center opened in 1970, after 8 years of construction by 10,000 workers.

- The south tower was 1,362 feet tall; the north tower was 1,368 feet tall. Their combined weight was 1.5 million tons.

- The entire complex contained 12 million square feet of office space on 16 acres in lower Manhattan. It used 68 miles of steel and 425,000 cubic yards of concrete, enough to lay a five-foot wide sidewalk from New York City to Washington, D.C.

THE WAR ON TERRORISM

- From September 11 to January 31, the "incremental cost" of the war on terrorism — what the Pentagon had to buy above and beyond its 2001 budget — was $10.717 billion.

- The estimated cost of the war in Afghanistan, called Operation Enduring Freedom, was $1 billion per month.

- On October 7, the first day of American and British bombing of Afghanistan involved 15 land-based bombers, 25 strike aircraft from carriers and 50 Tomahawk cruise missiles fired from warships. As many as 100 strike aircraft were involved in the heaviest days of bombing.

- To support the fighting in Afghanistan, the United States deployed 50,000 soldiers, sailors and airmen, three aircraft carrier groups and over 400 airplanes by early November. They were stationed in an arc from the Red Sea to the Indian Ocean. Twenty five thousand people were on naval vessels in the Arabian Sea. Three thousand troops were in Oman and 1,500 to 2,000 troops were in Uzbekistan.

- The cost of the deployment was $634 million.

- The number of United States forces in Afghanistan rose to around 7,000 in March 2002.

- As of December 25, 2001, approximately 17,000 operational sorties had been flown by U.S. planes.

- As of April 2, 2002, 22,434 bombs had been dropped on or fired at targets in Afghanistan.

- 60 percent of those weapons were precision guided, up from just 10 percent during the gulf war.

Hourly cost of operating U.S. aircraft:
- B-52 bomber: $86,000 per hour
- B-2 bomber: $137,000 per hour (B-2 missions in Afghanistan take up to 34 hours to complete)
- F-15 fighter: $4,500 per hour
- F-18 fighter $5,000 per hour

- Every Joint Direct Attack Munition-guided precision bomb costs about $25,000.

- Each cruise missile costs $1 million to $2 million. Eighty-eight were fired in the first two weeks of the bombing campaign.

- The largest bomb in the U.S. arsenal, the BLU-8, also called "Big Blue" or "daisy cutter," weighs 15,000 pounds.

The Taliban forces (estimate):
- Veteran core: 2,000 to 3,000
- Post-1995 adherents: 6,000 to 8,000
- Warlord, tribal and conscripted troops: 20,000 to 25,000
- Foreign volunteers 8,000 to 12,000 (5,000 to 7,000 Pakistanis; 1,500 to 2,000 Chechens and Uzbekistanis; 2,000 to 3,000 Al Qaeda fighters, mostly from Arab states)

- Estimated Taliban dead, as of mid-January: 3,000 to 4,000.

- Estimated: "Afghan Arab" dead, as of mid-January: 6,000 to 8,000.

- Approximately 7,000 Taliban and foreign troops were also taken prisoner.

- As many as 50,000 terrorists, from perhaps 50 countries, may have been trained by Al Qaeda in recent years. Since 1996, an estimated 20,000 recruits, from more than 20 countries, were trained at a dozen Al Qaeda training camps in Afghanistan.

- Between mid-September 2001 and mid-January 2002, an estimated 8,000 to 18,000 Afghan civilians fleeing the war zones died from starvation, exposure and related illnesses.

- The estimated number of civilian casualties caused by Operation Enduring Freedom is 1,000 to 4,000.

- An estimated 500,000 Afghan refugees and displaced persons were created by the U.S. bombing campaign.

- Between October 7 and December 3, 2001, 2,423,700 Humanitarian Daily Rations (HDR's) were dropped in Afghanistan, at a cost of approximately $51 million.

- As of March 5, 2002, Operation Enduring Freedom had resulted in deaths of 22 United States personnel (10 combat deaths, 12 accidental deaths).

- The number of allied Afghan militia deaths, as of mid-January 2002, was estimated at less than 600.

- The United States bombardment of Afghanistan has left an estimated 36,000 unexploded cluster bomb canisters on the ground in Afghanistan. Some 10 million to 15 million unexploded landmines remain in Afghanistan, left behind after the Soviet withdrawal.

- 136 countries had offered the United States military assistance in the war against terrorism by mid-January 2002.

- As of March 2002, $33 million in assets of 153 terrorists, terrorist organizations and financial centers was blocked by the United States. Another $33 million was blocked by other nations.

- Roughly 39,000 people received courses of antibiotics to protect them against possible anthrax exposure.

- Five people died of exposure to anthrax, which was mailed to media and government offices starting in mid-September 2001. The last to die, on November 2, 2001, was a 94-year-old woman in Oxford, Connecticut.

- The Health and Human Services Department said it would stockpile 300 million smallpox vaccination doses in case of a biological terrorism attack.

ECONOMICS

- The estimated total cost of planning and carrying out the September 11 attacks was $500,000.

- The estimated cost of The Tribute of Light, a temporary memorial at the World Trade Center site consisting of 88 searchlights, which projected two columns of light into the night sky for 33 days, is $500,000.

- The International Monetary Fund estimated the initial cost of September 11 to the United States at $21 billion.

- As of February 11, 2002, insurers had received $52 billion in claims arising from September 11.

- Approximately 100,000 people were laid off by the U.S. airline industry, as of September 21.

- On September 21, U.S. airlines received $15 billion in cash or federal loan guarantees to keep them in operation.

- The September 11 attacks are expected to cost the New York economy $83 billion by 2004.

- The city lost 125,000 jobs in 2001 because of the attacks, and is projected to suffer a net loss of 57,000 jobs by the end of 2003.

- In the 12 months following September 11, international tourism in New York is projected to fall 25%, costing the city $5 billion.

- The September 11 attacks will cost the United States an estimated 1.6 million jobs in 2002.

- Between September and December 2001, 30 U.S airport terminals were evacuated; 1,180 flights were delayed; 465 canceled and 15 diverted; passengers on 434 planes were ordered off for security rescreening.

- Domestic air travel was down 14 percent in December 2001 from the previous year; 19.8 percent in November; and nearly 40 percent immediately after September 11. By April 2002, it had nearly returned to normal.

- The September 11 attack disrupted more than 10,000 businesses in downtown New York, and displaced 377,000 workers.

- The four-star chef David Bouley prepared 1,547,496 meals for delivery to workers clearing the World Trade Center site, for a total fee of $5.8 million from the Red Cross.

- In addition to the buildings that were destroyed on September 11, 45 buildings, with a combined 10 million square feet of space, were seriously damaged. As of February 12, 2002, at least 22 were still closed.

AFGHANISTAN

- Total population (2001 est.): 26,813,057.

- Miles of paved road: 1,736 (2,793 km)

- Ethnic groups: 38 percent Pashtun; 25 percent Tajik; 6 percent Uzbek; 19 percent Hazara.

- By early 2000, 2 million Afghan refugees were living in Pakistan; 1 million to 1.4 million were living in Iran.

- Life expectancy: Male, 46.97 years; Female, 45.47 years.

- Infant mortality: 147.02 out of 1,000 live births, the fourth-highest rate on earth.

- One-quarter of Afghan children die before the age of 5.

- 31.5 percent of Afghans over 15 are literate.
- Male literacy: 47.2 percent; Female literacy: 15 percent.

- The cost of rebuilding Afghanistan in the next five years is estimated to be $9 billion.

• • •

- In a February 27 Gallup Poll conducted in nine Muslim nations — Indonesia, Iran, Jordan, Kuwait, Lebanon, Morocco, Pakistan, Saudi Arabia and Turkey — 61 percent said Arabs were not responsible for the September 11 attack.

- In the same poll, 9 percent said U.S. military action in Afghanistan was justifiable.

—COMPILED BY PETER EDIDIN

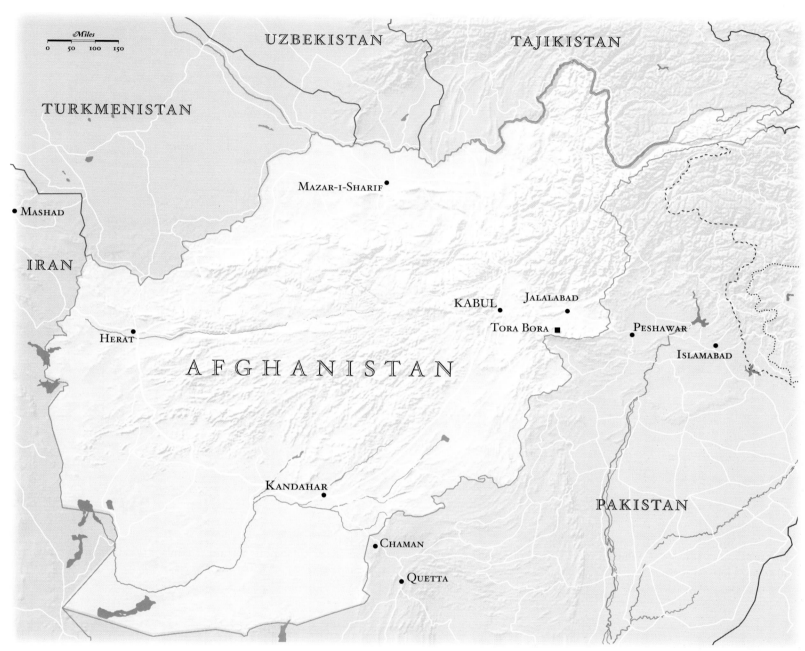

TURKMENISTAN

UZBEKISTAN

TAJIKISTAN

Miles
0   50   100   150

Mashad

IRAN

Mazar-i-Sharif

Herat

AFGHANISTAN

KABUL   JALALABAD

TORA BORA

PESHAWAR

ISLAMABAD

Kandahar

PAKISTAN

Chaman

Quetta

ACKNOWLEDGMENTS

The pictures and text in this book are part of the Pulitzer Prize-winning journalism produced by The New York Times since September 11, 2001. All of us — Lonnie Schlein, Mike Levitas, the editors at Callaway Editions and I — found it excruciating to choose from the deep and remarkable well of work. We would like to thank everyone for making our job so difficult.

The Times's mission is to enhance society. And so it did, in spite of the escalating costs of coverage, producing a vital, focused, Pulitzer-winning section, "A Nation Challenged," that also made possible this book. Though the story was told on the back of a great tragedy, we hope this book brings honor to the memory of the lost, including many within the Times family.

The text provides a perspective to the images and has been abridged from its original form for reasons of space. A few corrections also have been made. This history could not have been told (even in a picture book) with photos alone. Our writers' keyboards were like cameras, allowing readers to see and understand the story as it happened. We hope the abridgements do justice to their outstanding reporting.

Thank you, Howell Raines and Gerald Boyd, for believing in the power of photography. It made all the difference.

The men and women of the Picture Desk — led by Margaret O'Connor, Mike Smith and Jim Wilson — worked tirelessly, from the lab technicians to senior managers. This story crossed boundaries of foreign, national and metro news, and therefore crossed the desks of many talented picture editors, including Steve Berman, Pancho Bernasconi, Jeremiah Bogert, Cecilia Bohan, Karen Cetinkaya, Liz Claus, Beth Flynn, Philip Gefter, Stella Kramer, Kevin Larkin, Jose Lopez, Merrill Oliver, Lonnie Schlein, and Sarah Weissman. Of course, in the end, it was the photographers who brought the vision home. Many worked at grave risk, both here and abroad, to document the story of this horrid day and its aftermath. To all of them, staff and freelance, we express our gratitude and admiration.

Many ordinary citizens, badly shaken by what they had seen on September 11, also brought their pictures to our office. Thank you, accidental news photographers, for entrusting your record of history to us.

Of course, we were not the only ones covering the story. The wire services — The Associated Press, Reuters and Agence France-Presse — worked side by side with us throughout the months of newsgathering. We would like to thank their leadership for allowing us the privilege of publishing the work: Vin Alabiso of The A.P., Mitch Koppelman of Reuters and Maria Mann of A.F.P.

Charles Blow and Gentry Sleets did an amazing job of adapting the original graphics to a book format. Thanks, too, to the Times News Services staff for its hard work and encouragement: Tom Carley (our boss and advocate), Jim Mones, Phyllis Collazo, Peter Simmons, Merrill Perlman and Mitch Belitz.

And to our publishing partners at Callaway Editions, who worked on this book with a journalistic fervor, we give special thanks. Nicholas Callaway, George Gould, Carol Hinz, Toshiya Masuda, Antoinette White and the rest of the staff were true believers. They did a rough cut from nearly a thousand pictures, and we could not have done a better job ourselves. For these and other acts of publishing heroism, we hereby confer upon them the title of Honorary Times Journalist.

NANCY LEE
APRIL 22, 2002
NEW YORK CITY

The New York Times was awarded six 2002 Pulitzer Prizes for its commentary and coverage of 9/11, its victims, its causes and its aftermath. The awards are:

FOR PUBLIC SERVICE — Awarded for "A Nation Challenged," a special section published regularly that covered the events of September 11, profiled the victims and tracked the developing story, locally and globally.

FOR EXPLANATORY REPORTING — Awarded to the staff for its reporting, before and after the attacks, that profiled the global terrorism network and the threats it posed.

Stephen Engelberg • Judith Miller • James Risen • Kate Zernike
Don Van Natta Jr. • Douglas Jehl • Steven Erlanger • Chris Hedges
Jeff Gerth • Craig Pyes

FOR INTERNATIONAL REPORTING — Awarded to Barry Bearak for his coverage of daily life in war-torn Afghanistan.

FOR COMMENTARY — Awarded to Thomas L. Friedman for his reporting and commentary on the worldwide impact of the terrorist threat.

FOR BREAKING NEWS PHOTOGRAPHY — Awarded to the staff for its photographic coverage of the terrorist attack and its aftermath in New York City.

Suzanne DeChillo • Angel Franco • Ruth Fremson
Edward Keating • Chang W. Lee • Keith Meyers
Andrea Mohin • Krista Niles • Nancy Siesel • Kelly Guenther
George M. Gutierrez • Justin Lane • Steve Ludlum
Brian Manning

FOR FEATURE PHOTOGRAPHY — Awarded to the staff for its photographs chronicling the pain and the perseverance of the people of Afghanistan and Pakistan.

Stephen Crowley • Ruth Fremson • James Hill • Vincent Laforet
Chang W. Lee

1983.   FRED R. CONRAD/NYT

Published by Jonathan Cape 2002
1 3 5 7 9 10 8 6 4 2

First published in Great Britain in 2002 by Jonathan Cape, Random House,
20 Vauxhall Bridge Road, London SW1V 2SA

The Random House Group Limited Reg.No.954009
www.randomhouse.co.uk

ISBN 0-224-06964-0

Produced by Callaway Editions, Inc., New York

Nicholas Callaway, Editorial Director
Antoinette White, Senior Editor • Sarina Vetterli, Assistant Publisher
George Gould, Production Director • Toshiya Masuda, Art Director
Carol Hinz, Associate Editor • Ivan Wong Jr. and José Rodríguez, Design and Production

Back of jacket photograph: Vincent Laforet/NYT

Printed in the U.S.A.

The body text in this book is Hoefler Text, a family of typeface designs which was originally developed for Apple Computer from 1991 to 1993. The display type is Hoefler Titling, designed in 1996 to complement the Hoefler Text series. Both faces were inspired by sources such as Jean Jannon's Garamond No. 3 and Nicholas Kis' Janson Text 55. The title type is Champion Gothic, which was designed for *Sports Illustrated* in 1990. It is based loosely on a style of sans serif wood type which flourished in the late nineteenth century. All fonts were designed by The Hoefler Type Foundry Inc.

Cover image of The New York Times Magazine. September 23, 2001.

TRIBUTE IN LIGHT

After September 11, The New York Times Magazine asked the artists Julian LaVerdiere and Paul Myoda to conceive a memorial that could be used on the cover of the September 23 issue, which was to be entirely devoted to the tragedy. A digital representation of their idea, developed by them and the Times photographer Fred R. Conrad, was the result.

On March 11, 2002, two beams of light soared into the night sky near the World Trade Center site, memorializing the loss of the twin towers and all those who perished in the terrorist attack. This "Tribute in Light" brought to fruition the work first glimpsed on the September 23 Magazine cover, and included the efforts of other artists who had simultaneously been working on a similar idea.